WHAT YOU NEED TO KNOW ABOUT TODAY'S WORKPLACE:

A SURVIVAL GUIDE FOR NURSES

LYNDIA FLANAGAN

Lyndia Flanagan is an experienced writer and consultant. While employed with the American Nurses Association, Ms. Flanagan wrote a number of major publications, including *One Strong Voice, The Story of the American Nurses Association* (1976); *Entering and Moving in the Professional Job Market: A Nurse's Resource Kit* (1988); and *Self Employment in Nursing, Understanding the Basics of Starting a Business* (1993).

The views and opinions expressed in this book are solely those of the author. Nothing in this book is intended to be legal advice on any specific factual situation and readers are urged to contact their own attorneys with specific legal questions.

Published by
American Nurses Publishing
600 Maryland Avenue, SW
Suite 100 West
Washington, DC 20024-2571

ISBN 1-55810-101-2

EC-151   7.5M   6/95

CONTENTS

INTRODUCTION

The need for more sophisticated and complex health care services is increasing . . . . Consumer attitudes and expectations regarding delivery of care are increasingly demanding . . . . Health care providers continue to be locked into fierce competition with one another for scarcer and scarcer financial resources . . . . There is growing awareness among the public that certain populations lack access to adequate health care . . . . The body of scientific knowledge is expanding at such an accelerated rate that practitioners must constantly broaden their knowledge base and refine their skills . . . . Innovations in medical technology continue to produce new and improved lifesaving procedures.

The health care industry is responding to a variety of elements that have an impact on the structure of delivery systems, the composition and utilization of the workforce, and the nature and location of services. Changes within the industry are placing growing pressures on every nurse. Novice and experienced nurses alike must cultivate some very unique workplace skills in addition to clinical expertise. Clearly, the challenge is to become more business-minded professionals, more effective leaders in the workplace, and more discerning employees.

The purpose of this book is to address the realities of the workplace—to put into perspective the challenges each nurse faces in an industry undergoing dramatic changes. It provides an overview of the type of practical skills and information necessary to function effectively and successfully. It is intended to help today's nurse thrive in any type of work environment—be it threatening or filled with opportunity.

At first glance, the range of issues and concerns covered in this book may seem overwhelming. It must be emphasized, however, that knowledge and insight hold the key to experiencing a greater sense of control in the workplace. *What You Need to Know about Today's Workplace: A Survival Guide for Nurses* offers a broad look at what is happening within the industry, helping nurses to see beyond their immediate workplaces toward the bigger picture. It focuses on cultivating important skills that contribute to stress management and conflict resolution and facilitate effective communication. And it references valuable sources of information and support.

In the five short years since publishing the first edition, *Survival Skills in the Workplace, What Every Nurse Should Know*, there have been tremendous changes in the nurse's work environment. As a result, much new and updated material has been added. The first edition was structured around 30+ key questions; this new edition explores more than 70 pertinent concerns.

Nurses are encouraged to view this publication as an important resource, exploring those topics and/or specific questions that seem most relevant to an immediate situation. Taken together, the entire content lays the foundation for what every nurse should know about survival skills in the workplace.

L.F.

1

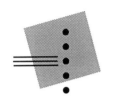

STAY APPRISED OF TRENDS IN THE INDUSTRY

It is an era of change for health care organizations and . . . an
era of opportunity for nursing as well as an era of challenge.

BARBARA J. STEVENS
The Nurse as Executive[1]

Today, there is a need for a new type of workplace savvy. Organizational restructuring and work redesign are occurring in all industries. And every worker is learning to cope with change.

Workers at all levels are looking beyond job titles, position descriptions, and corporate affiliation for a sense of career identity and purpose. The workplace is increasingly knowledge-driven and information-intensive. There is greater diversity within the workforce, compounding workplace relationships and group dynamics.

The health care industry and nursing, in particular, are a microcosm of what is happening in society. As one source notes, "In every industry, the business theories that drive decisions eventually become obsolete . . . personal computers are replacing mainframes and managed care is replacing the traditional fee-for-service model of delivering health care."[2] Both the industry at large and the local workplace are responding to economic, social, and political forces that necessitate restructuring of the health care industry. Changes in the organization, financing, and delivery of services pose tremendous challenges and opportunities for nurses.

As the twenty-first century approaches, it is essential that nurses become more sophisticated about survival and growth in an industry playing under new ground rules. A key ingredient in this process is cultivating an awareness of the trends affecting the industry. The purpose of this chapter is to offer an overview of several factors influencing the delivery of care and the roles nurses play. Major themes touched upon briefly in this chapter are explored at greater length in other sections of the book.

INDUSTRIALIZATION OF HEALTH CARE

The decade of the 1980s will be remembered as a period of dramatic transformation in health care, especially within the hospital industry. The introduction of Medicare's prospective payment system, spiraling health care costs, and increasing market competition made it necessary for hospitals to seek out more innovative ways to compete in the marketplace. Once passive payers of health services, the government and employers became major, aggressive purchasers. This change in posture forced hospitals, in particular, to lower prices or lose market share. According to some experts, these and other trends signaled the "industrialization" of health care.

The need to strengthen market forces has lead many health care institutions to restructure (horizontally and vertically) and/or to diversify. As a result, nurses once employed by small, private hospitals find themselves working for national chains or regional, multiunit systems. In many instances, this is only one of many changes in the employer-employee relationship. Many hospitals have contracted with outside services to provide entire management teams or to oversee certain clinical services. Some hospitals have entered into arrangements in which two or more organizations share certain staff, services, and facilities. However, no matter what the arrangement, the objective has been the same—reduction of expenditures and increased productivity.

Changes in the demand for health care services have further compounded the challenges facing nurses and other health care workers. Alterations in population characteristics, scientific and technological advancements, changing disease patterns, and increasingly diverse lifestyles have resulted in demands for a type of health care that was virtually nonexistent 10 or 20 years ago.

Increased patient acuity and earlier discharges characterize the "sicker and quicker" reality of the prospective payment system. Individuals who are being hospitalized tend to be more seriously ill, yet their length of stay is shorter. Patients who would have been cared for in intensive care units only a few years ago are now assigned to regular medical-surgical units. And older patients, more critically ill than ever before, are requiring increased nursing skill and nursing time.

There also is general consensus within the industry that patients are acting more like customers and that this change represents a significant shift in the patient's power. Various samplings of nurses indicate that patients differ dramatically from those of just 5 years ago. According to these nurses, patients are more questioning, less trusting, more demanding of high-quality service and care, more willing to shop around, more cost-conscious, and quicker to sue.[3]

As health care costs have continued to rise, greater emphasis has been placed on the benefits of health promotion, disease prevention, and physical and mental health. Many hospitals-turned-health-care-centers have created new services oriented toward both disease prevention and health promotion.

RETOOLING STRATEGIES OF THE 1990s

More recent efforts for health care reform have been directed at workplace redesign. According to experts, hospitals have now entered a second phase of retooling. In the first phase, the focus was on developing an outpatient infrastructure. In the second, more complex, phase of retooling, hospital executives are said to be addressing critical structure issues, such as the organization of the physical plant, the role and the responsibilities of caregivers, and the process of administering decision making.[4]

Total quality management and continuous quality improvement (TQM/CQI), patient-centered care, and critical paths are among the strategies being used in retooling efforts. In TQM/CQI, the primary focus is management and clinical process improvement. The strategies include quality improvement teams, greater employee involvement in decision making (empowerment), and quantifiable targets. "Clinical resource redeployment" is the primary focus in patient-centered care and the primary strategies include patient care teams, employee cross-training, and reconfiguring ancillary services. In critical paths, the primary focus is clinical process improvement. The strategies include staff protocols and measurement of outcomes.[5]

While many employers claim to be instituting quality management measures, their efforts are really directed at cutting costs, not improving care. Little or no consideration is being given to safety or quality of patient outcomes. Clearly, the focus is on the bottom line. Unfortunately, there is growing evidence that, regardless of how health care is reformed, employers will continue to try to reduce costs and increase productivity.

Sources tracking changes in the workforce report that work redesign activities frequently lead to inappropriate use of nurses and other health care personnel. For example, unlicensed and inadequately trained personnel are being used to replace rather than augment nursing care. Nurses are being required to work in multiple specialty areas without adequate training and experience. Registered nurse staffing is being reduced below what is needed to provide care that meets professionally determined standards of practice. Nurses also are being required to perform duties of other departments in addition to nursing duties, thus detracting from the time available to meet patients' needs.[6] These and other alarming measures have prompted many groups to voice concern about the need to better educate the public about the role nurses play and their contribution to the delivery of quality care.

DEMOGRAPHIC CHANGES

According to sociologists, there are three demographic trends that will significantly affect population patterns and, in turn, force major changes in health care in the very near future. The first trend is the aging of the population. The population is getting older because of increased life expectancy and the large numbers of individuals born between 1946 and 1964 (nearly one-third of the population).

In terms of structure and financing, the current health care system continues to be geared to acute care of younger people. Long-term care is a secondary priority. Given the anticipated numbers of aging people, a variety of sources concur that there is a pressing need for noninstitutional models of care, where appropriate; for integrated programs that offer acute, chronic, and social services; for training of skilled gerontological physicians, nurses, and other providers; for meaningful health promotion and preventive care for aging people; and for a serious commitment to research on the diseases of aging. In addition, there is general agreement that there is a need to reform the financing of care for the aging.

A second trend is that the number of women will continue to grow and, as a result, the aging population will be increasingly female. According to analysts, the following five characteristics of women and aging hold particular significance for the health care system:

1. The female majority is concentrated in the upper age ranges.

2. Women tend to marry men older than themselves. As a result, most elderly men have a spouse living with them; most elderly women do not.

3. Women are more likely than ever to live alone as a result of the death of spouses, divorce, or staying single.

4. Elderly women are more likely than elderly men to live in poverty.

5. Women are apparently in poorer health than men and, therefore, use more care.[7]

A basic profile that emerges from these characteristics is that of an aging female majority at greater risk of illness, financial vulnerability, and social isolation. These women form the basis of the future hospital patient population. The changes that will be required for appropriate care of the elderly in general will also be needed for the care of women.

The third demographic trend is the growing heterogeneity of the population in the United States. Between 1980 and 1990, the overall population grew by 10%—the white population by 8%, the black population by 16%, the Asian/other population by 65%, and the Hispanic population by 44%.[8]

According to analysts, a more heterogeneous patient population presents several specific challenges. First, minority Americans have a greater risk of being poor. Secondly, minority Americans have a disproportionate risk of being uninsured. And, finally, many health status indicators for minorities are poorer than those for whites. Black infant mortality, for example, is twice as high; minority maternal mortality is three to four times as high. Hispanic Americans are more likely to have diabetes, high blood pressure, kidney disease, some cancers, and acquired immune deficiency syndrome (AIDS). Hypertension disproportionately affects Asian-American men.

Health care institutions are being encouraged to "think multiculturally" in terms of program design, services offered, and actual contact with patients. According to industry experts, new types of outreach will be necessary to acquaint immigrants with the health care system. Social workers, patient representatives, health educators, and others (including physicians and nurses) will need language skills and cultural sensitivity to deal with these new patients.

VERTICALLY INTEGRATED SYSTEMS OF THE FUTURE

While projected changes in demographics and other factors continue to signal the need for comprehensive reform, the fate of a national plan for health care reform remains uncertain. However, it is clear that individual health care institutions will continue to respond to factors that have an impact on the structure and location of delivery systems, the composition and utilization of the workforce, and the nature of services.

Trade magazines tend to mirror themselves after the industry they represent. Such is the case with the magazine of the American Hospital Association (AHA). In 1993, the scope and readership of *Hospitals* magazine was broadened and the publication was renamed *Hospitals & Health Networks.* According to an AHA spokesperson, the magazine has periodically changed its format "to reflect the growing complexity of the health care environment."[9] The latest alterations are reportedly in response to systems integration.

Many experts in the field now believe that vertically integrated regional delivery systems, emphasizing primary care and preventive medicine, will prove to be the best approach to providing care. Vertically integrated systems represent a dramatic shift in priorities. The shift from a "hospital" mind-set to a "health care system" mind-set involves several philosophical changes, including a change from focusing on "filling beds" to "providing care at the appropriate levels;" from "caring for an individual patient" to "accountability for the health status of defined populations;" from "coordinating services" to "actively managing quality."[10]

It is anticipated that most integrated systems will involve strategic alliances between hospitals, physicians, and other providers. It is predicted that over the next few years, in most metropolitan areas, four or five major regionally integrated delivery systems will provide the bulk of health care services.[11]

As integrated delivery systems evolve, it is likely that each system will be structured differently to meet varying community needs. However, experts do expect such arrangements to share certain commonalities. For example, they are likely to take on significant risk by providing care for a defined population for a fixed amount of funding. They are likely to develop a continuum of care, from preventive medicine to hospice, with a primary care network as a key ingredient. And they are likely to integrate all care offered, so that patients move through the system efficiently.[12]

NURSING AND THE COMPETITIVE EDGE

According to Clare Hastings et al., "the competitive edge necessary for success in today's health care environment is dependent on creative solutions to new challenges and fresh approaches to old problems."[13] This means that nurses must be prepared to initiate change as well as adapt to it.

In addition to clinical expertise, nurses must rely upon a broad range of new workplace skills and knowledge. They must be more business-minded and innovative professionals. To articulate nursing's role and the value of nursing services, nurses must understand the economic forces operating in the health care system. They must translate client needs and budget considerations into programs that ensure effective care, reasonable remuneration for caregivers, and profits for the institution.

Nurses are said to be at "the hub" of the health care delivery system. Nurses must understand the effects of cost-containment practices on patient care and on the workforce. They must influence workplace redesign efforts, using cost and patient outcome data to assure that the most appropriate staffing levels and skill mix are used.

Nurses must be prepared to assume team-building roles. No matter what the work setting or role, it is likely that nurses will find themselves more closely involved in some form of group decision making—as part of primary nursing or interdisciplinary care teams, work units, special task forces, and/or committees. Consequently, nurses must be able to apply basic knowledge from the behavioral sciences to enhance interpersonal communication, foster team work, minimize stress, and facilitate problem solving and conflict resolution in the workplace.

Finally, nurses must become more discerning about employment options, work environments, and new and emerging roles. It is crucial for nurses to cultivate an awareness of the breadth of potential opportunities in nursing. For example, as patient populations continue to change, hospital nursing will pose new and different challenges, requiring greater innovation on the part of nurses. Restructuring activities also are opening up exciting opportunities in new and different health care settings. As a result, nurses may seek employment in a variety of worksites.

SUMMARY

As the twenty-first century approaches, a new and different type of workplace is emerging. Staying apprised of the trends in the industry is key to understanding how the work environment is changing. If nurses wish to experience a greater sense of control and satisfaction in the workplace, they will need to embrace a unique set of skills and knowledge. It will become increasingly important for nurses to exercise employment rights and protections, know the employer and the terms and conditions of employment, understand the work environment, scrutinize involvement in workplace decision making, recognize stress and its manifestation in the workplace, learn to manage workplace conflicts, and prepare for the future. The remainder of this book explores these important areas.

2

EXERCISE
EMPLOYMENT RIGHTS
AND PROTECTIONS

Virtually all workers and their employers are directly affected by the laws that extend to all types of jobs and all aspects of employment and, indeed, affect most working men and women from the time before they are hired until after they retire.

JAMES W. HUNT
The Law of the Workplace: Rights of Employers and Employees[14]

Experts contend that workplace problems often arise because of an employee's misunderstanding, lack of communication, and/or ignorance of workplace regulations. As employed professionals, nurses must be familiar with employment rights and protections. The first step toward asserting legal rights is to know what they are.

COMMON EMPLOYEE CONCERNS ABOUT WORKPLACE LAWS AND REGULATIONS

All employees are accorded certain rights and protections under state and federal laws. There are statutes and regulations pertaining to a wide range of employment concerns, including minimum wage; unemployment and disability benefits; equal employment opportunity; sex discrimination; unfair labor practices; collective bargaining; job safety; retirement, pensions, and social security; and government employment.

According to Hunt, many employers and employees are unfamiliar with the extent to which various laws affect their rights and responsibilities.[15] Consequently, it is important for nurses to have a knowledge of current workplace laws, as well as the specific statutes and regulations governing nursing practice. More importantly, it is critical that nurses have a clear understanding of the interrelationships between basic workplace laws, state nursing practice acts, and administrative rules within a specific employment setting.

Workplace laws and regulations are continuously evolving. Every year, Congress and the state legislatures make changes in legislation—ranging from modifications of existing statutes to enactment of new laws. Litigation also has an impact on the interpretation of specific legislation and regulations. As a result, it is impossible to present a comprehensive overview of all relevant employment law.

This chapter focuses on common employee questions likely to be of interest to nurses. (Sources of information on these and other relevant topics are discussed in the Appendix.) A wide variety of factors, however, may influence employment rights and protections in a given setting. Consequently, it is best to seek expert advice as specific issues arise.

At-Will Employment

What does employment at-will mean?

The vast majority of employment relationships are entered into for an indefinite period of time. There either is no employment contract or the contract makes no mention of the job's duration. This type of employment relationship is referred to as employment-at-will.

Under this arrangement, an employee can resign at any time for any reason. Likewise, an employer can terminate an indefinite employment arrangement by discharging the employee at any time for any reason, or for no reason at all—provided the employer does not violate any employment contract, bargaining agreement, or law restricting the circumstances in which the employee can be terminated. In recent years, however, at-will termination by employers has been subjected to a growing number of legal challenges. State legislatures also are taking steps to protect the rights of at-will employees.

For example, there have been an increasing number of lawsuits brought against health care institutions by at-will employees, on the basis of provisions in employee handbooks and personnel manuals, or other written policies of the institution. In a number of these cases, the courts have found that the employees have quasicontractual rights based on statements made by the employer. In a number of states, employers also have been held liable for discharging at-will employees when the termination was found to have violated public policy. Public policy refers to those policies governing public health, safety, or welfare established by constitutional provision, statute, or administrative rule.

(Other types of employment arrangements are discussed briefly in Chapter 3.)

Collective Bargaining

What rights and protections are accorded to nurses who wish to organize for collective bargaining purposes?

The National Labor Relations Act (NLRA), as amended by the Labor-Management Relations Act, is the federal law governing labor relations in the private business sector. Section 7 of the NLRA states that employees have the right to self-organize; to form, join, or assist labor organizations; and to bargain collectively through representatives of their own choosing.

Since the enactment of the National Labor Relations Act in 1935, employees of private, for-profit health care institutions have had the legal right to organize for collective bargaining purposes. Under the provisions of the NLRA, as amended in 1974, employees of voluntary, not-for-profit health care institutions also were granted the same rights and protections.

Over the years, there has been considerable debate over the composition of bargaining units in the health care industry. In March 1989, for the first time in the agency's history, the National Labor Relations Board (NLRB) voted to use its administrative rule-making authority to determine appropriate bargaining units in the health care industry. The Board issued rules finding appropriate eight bargaining units in private sector acute care facilities. The units were: registered nurses, physicians, professionals except for registered nurses and physicians, technical employees, skilled maintenance employees, business office clerical employees, guards, and other nonprofessional employees.

This decision followed 15 years of application of different standards and criteria by the NLRB and courts as well as extensive litigation over bargaining unit composition in health care facilities. As a result of litigation to delay implementation of the rules, the issue of the Board's authority to engage in rule-making ultimately reached the U.S. Supreme Court. In April 1991, a unanimous Supreme Court upheld the NLRB's use of its rule-making authority in this area. This paved the way for the implementation of the rules finding appropriate eight bargaining units, including one limited in composition to registered nurses.

Unfortunately, a more recent U.S. Supreme Court decision poses new issues and concerns regarding nurses' rights to engage in collective bargaining. In May 1994, a sharply divided U.S. Supreme Court ruled that nurses who direct the work of others may be considered to be supervisors and thus are not protected under the National Labor Relations Act. The ruling reverses a 20-year holding of the NLRB.

In the case of *National Labor Relations Board v. Health Care & Retirement Corporation of America*, the Court rejected the NLRB's argument that a nurse is not a supervisor when directing the work of others in the exercise of professional judgment and incidental to patient care. In the majority opinion, written by Justice Anthony M. Kennedy, the Court reasoned that a nurse who directs the work of an aide in caring for a patient is acting in the interest of the employer.

The Supreme Court's ruling is not a blanket determination. The NLRB will continue to do a case-by-case analysis of the work nurses do. Given the ruling, however, the Board must now determine supervisory status based on whether a nurse is acting as a "professional employee" (and thus covered by the Act) or as a front-line manager (and thus not covered).

The American Nurses Association has prepared a 20-page pamphlet, *How to Organize a Collective Bargaining Unit*, which provides in-depth information on organizing a collective bargaining unit through a state nurses association. More specific information may also be obtained from those state associations serving as bargaining agents.

Privacy Rights in the Workplace

To what extent does an employee have the right to privacy in the workplace?

An employee's privacy is largely affected by an employer's right to obtain information about the people it hires. This need for information is considered reasonable when it relates to the employer's interest in knowing about an employee's competence, reliability, and honesty as a worker or when required by the government to obtain information about a worker.

While there are limitations placed on an employee's right to privacy, there also are limitations on intrusion on that right. For example:

- An employer can contact an employee's previous employer for information about the individual's work history, as well as contact any references provided by the employee. However, if the employer intends to ask for an *investigative report* about the employee from a consumer reporting agency, the federal Fair Credit Reporting Act requires the employer to notify the employee and provide a copy of the report upon request.

- An employer has the right to *search* an employee's clothing or possessions for the theft of company property. However, if the circumstances of the employee's detention are unreasonable, the employer may be liable for false imprisonment.

- The Polygraph Protection Act of 1988 prevents most private employers from using *lie detector tests* to screen job applicants or to test current employees. Under the provisions of this act, employers are prohibited from disciplining, discharging, discriminating against, or denying employment or promotions to prospective or current workers solely on the basis of lie detector test results.

  Employers may request that an employee submit to a lie detector examination during an investigation of a workplace theft or other incident that causes economic loss or injury to the employer if: (1) the employee had access to the property under investigation; (2) the employer has a reasonable suspicion the employee was involved; and (3) the employer provides the employee with a written statement giving its reasons for testing particular employees. The law does prescribe detailed procedures that employers must follow during any permitted lie detector tests.

  The law permits private security firms and drug companies to continue administering lie detector tests to job applicants and employees. Federal, state, and local government employers are exempt from the ban.

A growing number of states have expanded their civil rights acts or enacted special legislation to prohibit an employer from requiring an employee or applicant to take a human immunodeficiency virus (HIV) *test* as a condition of employment or from using the fact that an employee has obtained an antibody test to affect the terms and conditions of employment or to fire the employee.

Moreover, if an applicant meets the definition of disabled under the Americans with Disabilities Act, an employer is prohibited from requiring pre-employment or pre-offer HIV tests or to ask specific questions about an applicant's HIV status. (Refer to the section "Disability Protections" in this chapter.) After a conditional job offer has been made, an employer may ask questions or require a test. If the test results are positive, however, the employer may not withdraw the offer unless it can be shown that the individual poses a direct threat that could not be eliminated by reasonable accommodation.

Over the past few years, there has been a significant increase in the number of employers who have instituted *drug-testing* programs for their employees. Most employer crackdowns on workplace drug abuse used to be voluntary actions on the part of management. Now, however, a wide range of employers are subject to stringent regulations aimed at eliminating the use of illegal drugs on the job.[16] For example, federal anti-drug initiatives are set forth in the Drug-Free Workplace Act of 1988, as well as in U.S. Defense Department contract rules and U.S. Transportation Department regulations. The Drug-Free Workplace Act covers all organizations receiving federal contracts of $25,000 or more, all federal contracts awarded to individuals, and all recipients of federal grants.

Nurses and other health care workers are subject to calls for drug testing because of their professional responsibilities, their contact with narcotics and other controlled substances, and the recognized occupational hazards for nurses and other health care professionals. The American Nurses Association is on record as opposing random drug screening of health care workers. The Association has given qualified support to drug and alcohol testing of employees when there is a reasonable suspicion and objective evidence that job performance is or has been impaired by alcohol or drug abuse. The Association emphasizes, however, that employers must provide managers and supervisors with specific and objective guidelines for establishing a reasonable suspicion of drug-impaired job performance.

Recently, *electronic monitoring* has become a matter of growing controversy between employers and employees. There has been an expansion in the types and uses of monitoring as a result of changes in technology and the job environment. Methods of monitoring include gathering information on computer systems, reading electronic mail, accessing telephone communications, and using closed circuit television. According to employers, these measures are designed to gauge productivity, protect business secrets, and detect misconduct.

During the last three sessions of Congress, legislation has been proposed to provide worker protection against electronic surveillance, to prohibit secret monitoring, and to require employers to notify employees of any monitoring policies. Electronic monitoring legislation also has been under consideration in several state legislatures. To date, however, none of these bills has passed.

In testifying before a congressional subcommittee in June 1993, a spokesperson for the American Nurses Association addressed three factors of concern to nurses: the intrusive, invasive nature of electronic monitoring; the growth in technology that will continue to make new forms of monitoring available; and the added stress to employees who are subjected to electronic monitoring.[17] ANA's testimony included the following observations:

It is imperative that federal law protect workers' rights to privacy. Currently, protection for an individual's right to privacy is unevenly reflected in our laws, and sadly absent from laws governing workplace policies and practices.[18]

Whistleblowers

Are there specific protections for whistleblowers?

Whistleblowers are employees who disclose information about an agency's violation of a law, rule, or regulation; mismanagement; gross waste of funds; abuse of authority; or a substantial and specific danger to public health or safety. Laws governing whistleblowing are a "patchwork of state and federal policy."[19] Legal protections may vary, depending on the activity reported and where the whistleblower is employed.

In general, whistleblower protection laws prohibit various methods of retaliation against employees who engage in whistleblowing. Although the specific kind of prohibited retaliation varies under the various laws, most laws prohibit actual discharge. In addition, most laws prohibit any negative changes in whistleblowers' terms and conditions of employment. Many laws also protect whistleblowers who are not dismissed, but who are forced to resign because the employer has created intolerable working conditions in retaliation for disclosure. An employee who fails to report improper practices through the employer's internal channels also may be protected.

Whistleblowers may be required to make their disclosures in good faith, to have reasonable cause to believe a violation has occurred or is about to occur, to make reasonable attempts to ascertain the correctness of their information, and to not make charges knowing they are false. Employees who knowingly make false charges may be subject to discipline. Moreover, a whistleblowing employee is not protected if he or she wrongfully discloses information that is classified, required to be kept secret in the interest of national security, or covered by the federal Privacy Act.

Although provisions to strengthen whistleblower protections are routinely introduced into Congress and the states, gaps in coverage still exist, leaving millions of workers vulnerable. In 1989, for example, Congress enacted the Whistleblower Protection Act to protect federal workers. This law, however, does not cover private sector, state, or local government employees. Given the limits in current federal and state whistleblowing laws, nurses should be advised that they may not be protected against retaliation for reporting unlawful, incompetent, or unsafe practices.

What protections are accorded employees under the First Amendment (right to free speech)?

Under the provisions of the First Amendment, government employees are afforded limited protection for matters of public concern. It is worth noting that, in May 1994, the U.S. Supreme Court issued a decision in a speech case involving a nurse. A four-justice plurality held that courts, in determining whether an employee was fired for protected speech on a matter of public concern, should "look to the facts as the employer reasonably found them to be," rather than determining those facts for itself.[20]

According to some sources, the ruling sets "new guidelines on how courts should handle disputes over the free speech rights of public employees."[21] Interestingly, the case (*Waters v. Churchill*) arose from a nurse's claims that a public hospital violated her First Amendment rights because it fired her after she spoke out on a matter of public concern: heightened patient risk due to inadequate training. The case was remanded back to the lower court for a decision on the issue of whether the employee was fired for making unprotected statements or for protected speech.

Overtime Pay

Is an employer obligated to pay overtime?

The Fair Labor Standards Act (FLSA) is the federal law that governs wages and hours of work. The FLSA sets minimum wage and overtime pay rates.

If an employee is classified as an administrative, professional, or executive employee and is *salaried*, that individual is generally *exempt* from FLSA's overtime requirements. An employee who is *paid an hourly rate*, on the other hand, is usually *nonexempt* and must be paid overtime. The overtime rate is no less than one and one-half times regular pay for work in excess of 40 hours a week. The "more than 40 hours a week" overtime rule, however, may be waived for hospitals and residential care establishments if there is a prior agreement or understanding with employees that overtime will be calculated over 14 days instead of the usual 7 days. Sometimes referred to as an "8 and 80 arrangement," overtime is paid for working more than 8 hours a day or more than 80 hours in 14 days.

In a brochure entitled *How Do You Know if Your Paycheck Is Correct*, the American Nurses Association points out that a nurse can receive overtime pay for:

- *On-call time*—if the calls are so frequent or conditions so restrictive that a nurse cannot use the time effectively for personal purposes, or if a nurse is required to report to work within a short time after being called. However, a nurse is not entitled to overtime pay if he or she is not required to remain on the premises, but merely needs to leave word where to be reached.

- *Time away from the worksite*—if the nurse is performing functions related to his or her job (e.g., phoning patients, families, physicians, or other providers) and if the employer knows or has reason to know the work is being done.

- *Nonproductive time*, such as changing into required scrubs, traveling to a required class, or lunchtime—if the nurse is required to stay in the unit on-call to work.[22]

It is the policy of many institutions to require supervisors to preapprove overtime. Failure to do so may warrant discipline. However, even if overtime is not formally requested and approved, overtime pay is owed if the supervisor was aware that the nurse was working. Supervisors may not change time cards or sheets to discount overtime if they accept the benefit of the work.[23]

It also is worth noting that while exempt (salaried) employees do not earn overtime pay, they cannot be docked for hours not actually worked. For example, an administrative, professional, or executive employee's pay may not be reduced when work is not available; for absences of less than a day; for jury duty, attendance as a witness at a trial, or military service; or for minor disciplinary violations. Major safety violations, however, could result in a deduction from pay.[24] In short, under the provisions of the Fair Labor Standards Act, employees are entitled to fair compensation for the work they do whether they are paid a salary or by the hour.

Fringe Benefits

Are there any laws regulating the provision of fringe benefits, including pension plans?

Although most employers provide fringe benefit packages to their employees, federal and state laws do not require payment of fringe benefits, except for payments that have to be made on behalf of employees for social security, workers' compensation, and unemployment insurance, or when an employer is performing work under a government contract. However, there are a number of measures that address various aspects of employee benefit plans. For example:

- All states require employers that do provide health insurance to their employees to provide minimum benefits, usually by requiring coverage for pregnancy and newborn children.

- The federal Age Discrimination in Employment Act requires employers to offer workers 65 years of age or older the same health insurance coverage offered to young workers. Although a person becomes eligible for Medicare at age 65, individuals who continue to work at that age have the option of either accepting at no extra cost any health insurance coverage provided by the employer or electing to receive Medicare.

- Under provisions of the Consolidated Omnibus Budget Reconciliation Act of 1985 (COBRA), employers with 20 or more workers must offer to extend existing health insurance coverage for up to 18 months to employees who leave work for any reason (except termination for gross misconduct) and to those whose work hours are reduced. (Also refer to the section "Layoffs" in this chapter.)

- Title VII of the Civil Rights Act of 1964 prohibits discrimination between men and women with regard to their pay and fringe benefits, including pensions. Employers must provide the same retirement benefits to male and female retired workers, even though the cost to the employer of funding the program may be greater for one sex.

- The Tax Reform Act of 1986 has been labeled "a landmark tax-overhaul measure."[25] Among other things, the act calls for all benefit plans sponsored by employers to satisfy new nondiscrimination requirements, starting with plan years beginning in 1989. The act also includes numerous provisions significantly affecting retirement and deferred compensation plans, group health and welfare benefits, and executive compensation programs.

An employer is not required to provide a pension to its workers. However, if a pension plan is offered, it must meet minimum standards established by the Employee Retirement Income Security Act (ERISA), enacted in 1974. This act also prohibits an employer from discharging a worker to avoid paying pension benefits. There also are other measures affecting provision of pension benefits, including the following:

- In 1984, the Retirement Equity Act (REA) called for changes in private pension laws aimed at increasing working women's chances of earning a pension. The REA (1) lowered from 25 to 21 the age at which employers must allow workers to participate in a pension plan, (2) lowered from 22 to 18 the age at which employers must count service once the worker belongs to the pension plan, (3) liberalized the treatment of workers who experience a break in continuous service (if a worker returns to the employer within 5 years, the pension credits earned before leaving employment are not lost, and (4) required that survivor benefits are automatically provided to the spouse of a worker who is vested when he or she dies, unless both spouses agree in writing to waive this protection.

- A number of retirement plan rules, including vesting, were affected by the provisions of the Tax Reform Act of 1986. *Vesting* means that the plan will pay the employee a pension at a specified retirement age, even if the worker should leave the job before reaching retirement age. Under the provisions of the Tax Reform Act, plan participants must have a nonforfeitable right to 100% of their accrued benefits upon completion of 5 years of service. *Vesting* also may be phased in 3 to 7 years. As a condition of participation, plans may require that an employee complete a period of service of no more than 2 years. However, plans that base participation on more than one year of service must grant employees full and immediate vesting rights.

With the aging of the workforce, pension issues are receiving greater attention. For example, Congress recently considered portable pension legislation. The legislation provided a model for pension coverage and increased savings for retirement by requiring employers that do not currently have pension plans to establish voluntary salary deductions from their employees. The legislation also proposed a lowering of vesting requirements to one year of employment. While the legislation did not pass, experts agree that the pension reform concepts are viable.

The issue of pension portability is particularly significant for nurses. Nurses are among the employee groups most severely disadvantaged under current pension systems. Job mobility is a dominant employment characteristic of nurses. As nurses move from one employer to another during their careers, they are likely to be covered by various types of pension plans providing widely differing levels of benefits and settlement options.[26] When nurses change jobs, they can lose pension benefits they otherwise might have accumulated had they remained with a single employer. Pension portability would provide nurses with a pension that could be transferred over an entire career involving multiple jobs and employers. To this end, the American Nurses Association is investigating the viability of various approaches to portable pension plans.

Workers' Compensation

Are employees with job-related injuries or occupational diseases entitled to workers' compensation?

When employees suffer job-related injuries or contract an occupational disease, they must notify their employer and file for benefits within a specified period of time. In most states, employers are required to post notices informing their employees of these reporting and filing requirements.

Federal workers and certain other workers are covered by federal workers' compensation systems. Since each state operates its own system, however, the employees covered, the amount of compensation, duration of benefits, and procedures for making and settling claims vary widely. Consequently, it is important to obtain more specific information about compensation benefits and procedures in a particular situation.

Workers' compensation programs operate on a "no fault" system. An employer pays benefits to the employee for job-related injuries without regard as to who was at fault in causing the injury. In return, the employee forgoes the right to sue the employer. However, in the event that a worker's injury was caused by a third party (a defective product or faulty equipment, for example), the employee can collect workers' compensation from the employer as well as sue the third party for causing the injury. In a few states, employers can elect not to participate in the state's workers' compensation program. If they elect not to participate, they can be sued by their employees for job-related injuries.

Generally, workers' compensation programs provide payments to an injured worker for necessary medical expenses. In the event of death, they also pay benefits, including burial expenses, to the worker's family. There is no waiting period for necessary medical or hospital care. Most state laws do require a waiting period of three to seven days after a disabling injury before the payment of benefits for lost work time begins.

Most state workers' compensation laws provide for rehabilitation services for injured workers who, although unable to return to their former job because of an injury, can obtain other employment with medical care, counseling, guidance, schooling, or training. The federal Vocational Rehabilitation Act also provides funds for federal-state rehabilitation programs operated by a state's vocational rehabilitation department or agency.

Compensation payments are generally financed through private insurance companies, state compensation funds, or self-insurance by employers. On occasion, disputes may arise between an employee and program carrier over the payment of claims. If the parties are unable to resolve their differences, the case is referred to an impartial examiner, referee, or judge (depending on the state procedure) for a hearing and resolution of the dispute.

(Refer to the section "Bloodborne Diseases" in this chapter for a more specific discussion of workers' compensation issues related to bloodborne diseases.)

Layoffs

Is there any special assistance for individuals who are laid off?

The incidence of layoffs in the health care industry, particularly in hospital settings, is on the rise. According to researchers, one of the most frequently cited reasons that hospitals are reducing the numbers of full-time equivalent (FTE) registered nurse positions is workplace restructuring, which frequently involves cross-training, substitution, and/or work elimination.[27]

Given the current environment, it is important for all health care employees, including nurses, to be aware of several legislative provisions:

- In 1988, Congress enacted the Worker Adjustment and Retraining Notification (WARN) Act. Under the WARN Act, employers with 100 or more employees must give a written, 60-day notice of any planned large-scale layoff or closure that will last more than 30 days. The WARN Act requires employers to notify the affected workers or their representatives, the chief elected official of local government, and the state's designated worker unit. An employer who violates the WARN Act may be liable for back pay and benefits to the affected workers and be ordered to pay up to $500 in civil penalties for each day of violation.

In the spring of 1994, bills were introduced in the House and Senate to amend the WARN Act to lower the threshold for determining employer coverage from 100 or more employees to those with 50 or more (including part-time employees) and to set a sliding scale for the length of notification required. The American Nurses Association has indicated its support of such legislation. An association spokesperson noted, "Given that the health care system is going through monumental restructuring, legislation that gives nurses advance warning to pending job loss would be beneficial and appropriate."[28]

- Under civil rights laws, employers must monitor layoff ratios to ensure no discrimination against minorities, women, older workers, and other protected groups. The Older Worker Benefits Protection Act and Age Discrimination in Employment Act place restrictions on severance packages and notification rules pertaining to employees over 40 years of age.

- Under provisions of the Consolidated Omnibus Budget Reconciliation Act of 1985 (COBRA), all employers of 20 or more employees must offer to extend health care insurance coverage to employees who leave or have their work hours reduced. Benefits are continued under the plan that the employee was covered by at the time of termination for generally up to 18 months. This period may be extended depending upon events affecting the employee.

An employee must decide to continue coverage under the institutional plan within 60 days of the later of the following events: (1) coverage loss date or (2) date the notice to elect COBRA coverage is sent. It is important to note, however, that coverage is extended only to employees who are covered at the time of termination. An employee who was not using the organization's insurance plan would not be able to suddenly sign up.

An employee eligible for COBRA coverage must bear the full cost of coverage. The employer is no longer responsible for any of the costs. However, the premium paid by the employee is at the employer's group rate (plus up to 2 percent more to cover administrative costs), which generally is cheaper for the employee than trying to buy an individual health insurance policy after termination. Payment for coverage must be made within 45 days of electing COBRA coverage. If elected, COBRA coverage is retroactive to the coverage loss date.

There are also many state laws that contain continuation coverage provisions. The state law provisions may either parallel COBRA's requirements or they may be entirely different. These state laws do not apply to self-funded group health plans.

- Programs for dislocated workers are authorized under Title III of the Job Training Partnership Act. Many programs are industry-specific, designed for individuals who have lost their jobs because of acts of government (e.g., closure of military facilities).

  The Economic Dislocated Worker Adjustment Act (EDWAA) applies to dislocated workers who are unlikely to return to their previous industries or occupations. The program is designed to operate at the local level. Federal funds are made available to states on a formula basis.

  EDWAA benefits include an array of services designed to meet individual needs. Among the services offered are long-term job preparation. Training may include classroom instruction, occupational skills, and/or on-the-job training. EDWAA programs provide labor market information, job search and placement assistance, support services (including child care), and relocation assistance.

Recently, Congress began exploring a major overhaul of training and reemployment legislation. The goal of this reform is to consolidate federal job training programs and create a single comprehensive program, encompassing a number of elements.

Age Discrimination

Is there a law prohibiting age discrimination in employment practices?

Under the federal Age Discrimination in Employment Act (ADEA), it is unlawful to discriminate against persons between the ages of 40 and 70 in hiring, firing, pay promotions, fringe benefits, and other aspects of employment. The law prohibits the involuntary retirement of workers under age 70, except for certain senior executive and high-level policy-making employees. There is no upper age limit with respect to employment in the federal government. The ADEA applies to all public employers, private employers of 20 or more employees, employment agencies serving covered employers, and labor unions of more than 25 members.

Examples of age discrimination include:

- Indicating an age preference in "help wanted" advertisements,

- Classifying workers in such a manner that their employment opportunities would be adversely affected because of their age,

- Requiring a person to retire solely because of his or her age, and

- Using employee benefit plans as a basis for refusing to hire older applicants.[29]

An employer, however, may base employment consideration on a person's age when age is a bona fide occupational qualification for the normal operation of the business.

In addition to the federal law, many states have age discrimination laws or provisions in state fair employment practice laws that prohibit discrimination based on age. Some of these laws have no upper limits in protections against age discrimination in employment; other laws protect workers until they reach 60, 65, or 70 years of age.

The trend toward an older workforce is prompting both public and private groups to scrutinize the needs of older workers. Several years ago, the U.S. Department of Labor warned that employers must begin adjusting their personnel policies to address the economic realities of a workforce that includes an expanding number of older employees and fewer young, entry-level jobholders.[30] The department's Employment Standards Administration is addressing affirmative action efforts for an older workforce. Among the subjects that continue to be explored are job redesign, increased recruitment and training, flexible working hours, and changes in retirement policy.

Sexual Harassment

What constitutes sexual harassment in the workplace?

Since 1964, Title VII of the Civil Rights Act has prohibited discrimination in employment conditions because of race, color, religion, sex, or national origin. In 1976, it was acknowledged that Title VII also prohibits sexual harassment as a form of sex discrimination.

According to the Equal Employment Opportunity Commission (EEOC), the federal agency that enforces Title VII, unwelcome sexual advances, requests for sexual favors, and other verbal or physical conduct of a sexual nature constitute sexual harassment on the job when the following conditions exist:

- Submission to such conduct is made either explicitly or implicitly a term or condition of an individual's employment, or

- Submission to or rejection of such conduct by an individual is used as a basis for employment decisions, or

- Such conduct has the purpose or effect of unreasonably interfering with an individual's work performance or creating an intimidating, hostile, or offensive working environment.[31]

Under the law, there are two basic types of sexual harassment: quid pro quo ("this for that") and hostile environment. In quid pro quo sexual harassment, a violation of Title VII occurs when an individual uses his or her authority to extort sexual considerations from an employee. For example, it is unlawful for a supervisor to directly or indirectly condition a job benefit on the receipt of sexual favors from a subordinate or to punish that subordinate for refusing to comply with a request for sexual favors. A single, well-documented incident of this nature is often enough to prove a violation.

Unlawful hostile environment harassment may occur where there has been no tangible impact on job status, but where sexually harassing conduct on the job creates an abusive work environment or interferes with an employee's work performance. Unlike quid pro quo harassment, this form of sexual harassment may result from the actions of co-workers and nonemployees as well as supervisors. Moreover, it is not limited to sexual advances. It may involve nonsexual behavior directed at an individual because of gender.

According to one source, a sexually hostile work environment can be created by:

- Discussing sexual activities;

- Unnecessary touching;

- Commenting on physical attributes;

- Displaying sexually suggestive pictures;

- Using demeaning or inappropriate terms, such as "Babe";

- Using unseemly gestures;

- Ostracizing workers of one gender by those of the other;

- Granting job favors to those who participate in consensual sexual activity; or

- Using crude and offensive language.[32]

In a hostile environment situation, one isolated incident is rarely enough. To prove a violation of Title VII, the offensive conduct must be continuous, frequent, repetitive, and part of an overall pattern.

In a recent case (*Harris v. Forklift Systems*), the U.S. Supreme Court clarified the legal standard of harassment—to establish a violation of Title VII, the environment must be one that a reasonable person would find hostile or abusive, and the victim must perceive that the environment is abusive.[33] The Court set forth several factors to be considered in determining whether an environment is hostile or abusive. These factors include the frequency and severity of the conduct, whether the conduct is physically threatening or humiliating or a mere offensive utterance, and whether the conduct unreasonably interferes with an employee's work performance.

In addition to Title VII, there are other legal protections against sexual harassment. For example, Title IX of the Education Amendments of 1972 prohibits sex discrimination and sexual harassment in any educational program receiving financial assistance from the federal government. On the state level, employees may be protected under the fair employment statues that exist in almost every state. In addition, some state workers' compensation statutes provide remedies for employees who have been injured, either physically or psychologically by sexual harassment in the workplace. Prohibition against sexual harassment in the workplace also may be included in collective bargaining agreements.[34]

General guidelines for dealing with sexual harassment in the workplace are addressed in Chapter 4.

Pregnancy and Maternity Leave

Can women be discriminated against in employment-related matters on the basis of pregnancy, childbirth, or related medical conditions?

Title VII of the Civil Rights Act of 1964 is the principal federal employment discrimination law. As amended by the Pregnancy Discrimination Act of 1978, Title VII specifically prohibits discrimination on the basis of pregnancy-related conditions. Consequently:

- A female employee cannot be denied a job or a promotion solely because she is pregnant.

- A pregnant employee cannot be required to go on leave if she is able to do her job.

- If an employer provides health insurance to cover expenses for other medical conditions, health insurance coverage for pregnancy-related conditions must also be provided. Moreover, employers must provide such coverage for the nonworking wives of male employees if it is provided for female employees.

- A pregnant employee is entitled to maternity leave on the same basis that leave is granted to employees for other temporary disabilities. If she intends to return to work, her job must be held open on the same basis as jobs are held open for employees on leave for other disabilities.

- A female employee cannot be prohibited from returning to work for any arbitrary predetermined period following childbirth. On her return to work, she is entitled to fringe benefits and seniority on the same basis as other employees returning from leave for other disabilities.

It is also worth noting that in September 1989, in *Aubrey v. Aetna Life Insurance Company*, the U.S. Court of Appeals for the Sixth Circuit ruled that it is permissible for pregnant employees receiving prenatal care prior to their coverage under an employer's health benefit plan to be reimbursed for pregnancy-related expenses, even if employees who receive treatment for other "preexisting" conditions are not covered under the plan.[35]

In defending its plan, Aetna had argued that the Pregnancy Discrimination Act (PDA) does not permit more beneficial treatment of pregnancy-related conditions than other diseases or disabilities covered under an employer's health benefit plan. The court, however, rejected this interpretation. In writing for the court, Judge H. Ted Milburn stated, "The PDA prohibits discrimination; it does not prevent an employer from treating pregnant employees more beneficially than it treats other employees. As the Supreme Court has indicated, 'Congress intended the PDA to be a floor beneath which pregnancy disability benefits may not drop—not a ceiling above which they may not rise'."[36]

Family and Medical Leave

What are the provisions of the Family and Medical Leave Act?

The Family and Medical Leave Act of 1993 (FMLA) allows an employee to take up to 12 weeks of *unpaid* leave in a 12-month period (1) for the birth of a child; (2) to care for an employee's newborn, newly adopted child, or child newly placed in foster care; (3) to care for an employee's spouse, child, or parent with a serious health condition; or (4) to care for an employee's own serious health condition. The FMLA covers all private employers with 50 or more employees within a 75-mile radius, the Federal government, and the United States Congress.

To be eligible for leave under FMLA, an employee must have worked for the employer for at least one year and for at least 1,250 hours during the 12-month period immediately prior to the beginning of the leave period. Under provisions of the Act, an employee must provide the employer with 30 days advance notice or as much notice as practicable given the circumstances. The advance request for FMLA leave should be submitted in writing as a point of record. An employer may require medical certification to support a request for leave because of a serious health condition (that of a family member or an employee's own). An employer must tell an employee that medical certification is required at the time leave is requested.

The FMLA defines a serious health condition as one that requires either inpatient care or continuing treatment by a health care provider. Examples of serious conditions include heart attacks, heart conditions requiring heart bypass or valve operations, most cancers, back conditions requiring extensive therapy or surgical procedures, strokes, severe arthritis, severe nervous disorders, injuries caused by serious accidents on or off the job, severe morning sickness, childbirth, and recovery from childbirth.[37]

A serious health condition also is defined as one that renders an individual unable to attend work or school or perform other daily activities for more than three days and requires continuing treatment by a health care provider. Treatment for a serious, chronic health condition which, if left untreated, would likely result in an absence from work of more than three days also qualifies under the FMLA. Prenatal care is also included, but routine physical examinations are not included.[38]

Under the terms of the Family and Medical Leave Act, an employer must maintain health insurance benefits during the period of leave at the level and under the conditions coverage would have been provided if the employee had not taken leave. An employer can recover health insurance premiums paid during leave from an employee who does not return to work after leave, unless the employee cannot return to work because of a serious health condition (either a family member or an employee's own). Upon return from FMLA leave, an employee must be given his or her previous position or an equivalent position with equivalent employment benefits, pay, and other terms and conditions of employment. An employer, however, is not required to restore a salaried employee to the previous or equivalent position if the employee is among the highest paid 10 percent of the employees within a 75-mile radius of the employee's worksite.[39]

The FMLA makes it unlawful for any employer to interfere with, restrain, or deny the exercise of any right provided under the Act. Any employee who feels his or her rights have been violated can bring legal action in either federal or state court to recover damages (e.g., wages, employment benefits, or other compensation lost because of the violation); equitable relief (e.g., reinstatement, promotion); and reasonable attorney's fees, reasonable expert witness fees, and other costs. An employee's right to bring a private action ends, however, if the Secretary of Labor intervenes and brings a legal action on behalf of the employee.

Finally, it important to note that the Family and Medical Leave Act provides a MINIMUM floor to which an employer must adhere in the provision of leave and employee benefits during that leave. Any state or local law or collective bargaining agreement can make allowances for more generous family and medical leave provisions (rights).

Disability Protections

How is "disability" defined under the Americans with Disabilities Act?

The Americans with Disabilities Act (ADA) is civil rights legislation giving individuals with disabilities protection from discrimination in employment and in access to commercial facilities, transportation, telecommunications, and state and local government services.

Under the ADA, an individual with a disability is a person who has a physical or mental impairment that substantially limits one or more major life activities. Major life activities include caring for one's self, performing manual tasks, walking, seeing, hearing, speaking, breathing, learning, and working. For example, a person with epilepsy, paralysis, a hearing or vision impairment, a learning disability, or AIDS would be covered. Individuals with minor, short-term conditions, such as a broken bone, are generally not protected by the ADA; nor are individuals with minor problems that do not substantially limit major life activities. Other conditions that generally are not covered include physical characteristics (e.g., hair or eye color); personality traits; environmental, cultural, or economic disadvantages; and advanced age.

The ADA also protects people with a history of impairment, such as a cancer patient who is in remission, a person who is back at work after a heart attack, or a person with a history of mental illness. In addition, the act protects people who are perceived to have a disability, such as a person who is severely disfigured.

Not only does ADA protect individuals with actual or perceived disabilities, it also protects from discrimination workers who are associated with or have a relationship with a person with a disability. For example, an employer cannot refuse to hire the spouse of an individual with AIDS on the basis of that relationship.

There are certain conditions that are specifically *exempted* from coverage, including lifestyle choices, compulsive gamblers, kleptomaniacs, pyromaniacs, pedophiles, exhibitionists, and those with other sexual behavior disorders. Current illegal drug users are not protected by the ADA. However, former drug users who have been rehabilitated, who are participating in a supervised rehabilitation program and are not currently using drugs, or individuals who are erroneously regarded as using illegal drugs are protected by the law and may not be discriminated against. Alcoholics are covered under the ADA, but they must be qualified—able to safely perform the job.[40]

Under the employment provisions of the Americans with Disabilities Act (Title I), employers with 15 or more workers are prohibited from discriminating against "qualified" individuals in the recruiting, application, and hiring processes. A qualified individual with a disability is "one who has a disability, within the meaning of ADA, and who, with or without a reasonable accommodation, can perform the essential functions of the job."[41]

An employer also may not discriminate against a qualified individual with a disability in regard to any terms, conditions, or privileges of employment, including:

- Limiting, segregating, or classifying a job applicant or employee so as to adversely affect the opportunities or status of the individual;

- Participating in a contractual or other arrangement or relationship that subjects a qualified individual with a disability to discrimination;

- Using standard, criteria, or methods of administration that have the effect of discriminating;

- Using qualification standards, employment tests, or other selection criteria that screen out an individual or class of individuals with disabilities, unless the selection criteria is shown to be job-related; or

- Failing to make reasonable accommodation for a qualified individual with a disability, unless the employer can show that the accommodation would cause undue hardship on the operation of the business.

Any complaints about violations of the employment section of the Americans with Disabilities Act are to be filed with the Equal Employment Opportunity Commission.

Safe Work Environment

Are there regulations to protect employees from health and safety hazards in the workplace?

Employers are required by the Occupational Safety and Health Act of 1970 and by many state laws to maintain a safe and healthful workplace. The federal law is enforced by the Occupational Safety and Health Administration (OSHA). In addition to eliminating recognizable hazards, employers must also comply with specific OSHA-prescribed job safety and health standards. These standards cover such matters as fire protection, construction and maintenance of equipment, worker training, machine guarding, and protective equipment to be worn by workers. Employers are also required to familiarize themselves with and observe the OSHA standards applicable to their type of business and to inform their workers of these standards.

Under the Occupational Safety and Health Act, employees have a right to seek safety and health on the job without fear of punishment. Employees also have the right to:

- Review copies of appropriate OSHA standards, rules, regulations, and requirements that the employer should have available at the workplace;

- Request information from the employer on safety and health hazards in the area, on precautions that may be taken, and on procedures to be followed if an employee is involved in an accident or is exposed to toxic substances;

- Request the OSHA area director to conduct an inspection if it is believed that hazardous conditions or violations of standards exist in the workplace;

- Have an authorized employee representative accompany an OSHA official during any inspection tour;

- Respond to questions from an OSHA inspector; and

- Review employer information about job-related accidents and injuries in the workplace, as specified under the act.

(Refer to the Appendix for a listing of OSHA regional offices.)

Congressional support is being sought for comprehensive occupational safety and health reform. Legislation has been proposed to address what some experts describe as "education, enforcement, and regulatory gaps that have existed over 20 years since the current law's inception."[42] A major goal of reform legislation would be to extend the coverage of the Occupational Safety and Health Act to public sector employees. Proposed legislation also includes provisions to strengthen worker involvement in health and safety by requiring employers to develop health and safety standards and labor-management health and safety committees.

Over the past few years, OSHA has stepped up efforts to address many of the major concerns in the health care industry. It has issued a specific standard on bloodborne pathogens and is taking similar action to address tuberculosis. (Refer to the sections "Bloodborne Diseases" and "Tuberculosis" in this chapter.) The agency also is seeking nonregulatory avenues to address the health and safety needs of workers and employers, including education about violence in the workplace as a health and safety issue.

Hazardous Chemicals

Do employees have a right to know about hazardous chemicals in the workplace?

While there are a number of different federal and state regulations that apply to the handling of hazardous substances, OSHA's Hazard Communication Standard (HCS) is the primary federal right-to-know law. As a result of a U.S. Supreme Court decision in 1990, the provisions of this standard are now in effect in all industries, including the coverage of hazardous drugs and pharmaceuticals in the nonmanufacturing sector.

OSHA defines a hazardous chemical as any chemical that is a physical hazard or a health hazard. *Physical hazard* refers to a characteristic such as combustibility or reactivity. A *health hazard* is defined as a chemical for which there is statistically significant evidence based on at least one study conducted in accordance with scientific principles that acute or chronic health effects may occur in exposed employees.[43] Among the hazardous substances commonly found in hospitals are asbestos, antineoplastic drugs/cytotoxic agents, anesthetic agents, ethylene oxide (ETO), formaldehyde, solvents, and mercury.

The HCS requires chemical suppliers to evaluate the health effects of the chemicals they manufacture or import and provide this information to employers purchasing chemicals. The standard requires that:

- All hazardous chemical containers that enter the workplace must be labeled with the substance's effects.

- Employers must train workers who handle hazardous chemicals on the job. This training should include information on physical and health hazards of chemicals in the workplace, appropriate work practices, emergency procedures in the event of exposure, and use of personal protective equipment.

- A Material Safety Data Sheet (MSDS) must be available for each chemical. An MSDS must include information on all health effects of a chemical, including any known or suspected reproductive effects. Package inserts and PDR listings are not acceptable.

There are also several other OSHA standards that incorporate some of the components of the HCS, including ones for ETO and formaldehyde.

According to experts, a major shortcoming of existing safeguards is the failure to alert workers to any possible reproductive health effects from chemical and other exposures. While studies on the effects of workplace hazards on reproduction are limited, the National Institute for Occupational Safety and Health (NIOSH) views reproductive disorders as one of the 10 most frequent work-related diseases.[44] Nurses, in particular, are encouraged to "utilize all of the information and exposure prevention methods currently available in order to avoid unnecessary risks."[45] As one occupational safety and health specialist points out:

If you don't feel that you have received adequate information, especially about the potential reproductive effects of hazardous agents, you may need to contact an outside information source. Many states sponsor phone information lines known as teratogen information or pregnancy hotlines. Even your local poison control network may be of assistance.[46]

Bloodborne Diseases

What steps are being taken to reduce the occupational risks associated with bloodborne diseases?

As concerns about transmission of HIV and other bloodborne pathogens in health care settings grew in the 1980s, the Centers for Disease Control and Prevention (CDC) developed universal blood and body fluid precautions. These guidelines, referred to as "universal precautions," stress that *all* patients should be assumed to be infectious for HIV and other bloodborne pathogens. Caregivers are advised to handle all blood and body fluids as potentially infectious. While CDC does not have regulatory or enforcement authority, its guidelines are used as professional standards of practice. As a result, they are perceived by many as having mandatory status.

In 1992, under continued pressure from workers, OSHA's Standard on Occupational Exposure to Bloodborne Pathogens went into effect. The standard covers private sector and federal civilian employees. The Department of Veterans Affairs also has chosen to implement the standard's provisions. State, county, and municipal employees are not covered by the regulation.

Under this standard, hospitals and other health care employers with one or more employees are required, among other things, to:

- Develop an exposure control plan that includes identification of employees with potential for occupational exposure;

- Train all identified employees on occupational risks and methods to reduce risk;

- Provide voluntary hepatitis B vaccine at no cost to identified employees;

- Maintain records of employee training and medical evaluations;

- Use warning labels and signs to identify hazards;

- Implement methods to comply with provisions for worker protection, including universal precautions and the safe handling of sharps, specimens, contaminated laundry, and regulated waste;

- Provide medical evaluation and treatment after exposure incidents;

- Provide personal protective clothing and equipment; and

- Evaluate the effectiveness of current safety technology.[47]

A needlestick is the most obvious exposure incident. However, any specific eye, mouth, other mucous membrane, nonintact skin, or parenteral contact with potentially infectious materials is considered "an exposure incident." And it should be reported to the employer *immediately.*

The CDC has developed guidelines for the management of health care workers after occupational exposure to HIV. A comprehensive postexposure program should be in place in all health care settings. It should provide immediate evaluation, prophylactic interventions, counseling, and supportive care to any employee who has possibly been exposed to bloodborne pathogens.

Nurses must adhere to universal precautions and teach others to do so. Recent studies on HIV infection control document the need for all health care workers to improve the manner in which infection control and safety techniques are practiced.

It should be noted that universal precautions and the bloodborne pathogens standard are not the final answer in preventing life-threatening exposures. One of the most effective means of eliminating exposures is to eliminate unnecessary needles. The founder of the Exposure Prevention Information Network believes that the efforts of the health care worker and medical device communities must shift to utilization of needleless products. The bloodborne pathogens standard encourages, but does not mandate, the use of safer devices. Therefore, health care workers must be proactive in assuring such use in their own workplaces.

The American Nurses Association has compiled a brochure entitled *Bloodborne Diseases: Nurses' Risks, Rights, and Responsibilities.* The association has also published *Nursing and HIV/AIDS*, a 100-page book designed for nurses involved in direct practice, education, administration, research, and/or health policy, as well as for nursing students. (Also refer to the AIDS hotlines listed in the Appendix.)

What are the employment rights of health care workers who are HIV/HBV infected?

As discussed in a previous section of this chapter, the Americans with Disabilities Act prohibits discrimination in all employment practices against any person with a disability. Individuals with HIV/AIDS are covered under the provisions of this act.

While there are increasing efforts to prevent discrimination against HIV-infected employees, there is still some controversy regarding HIV-infected health care providers. Addressing the subject in *Nursing and HIV/AIDS*, an expert panel of the American Nurses Association made the following observations:

Nurses who know that they are HIV-infected should voluntarily avoid exposure-prone invasive procedures that have been scientifically linked to HIV or other bloodborne infection transmission. Self-restriction of practice must be decided on a case-by-case basis through consultation with the personal care provider and in keeping with guidelines from the CDC and state professional boards. Confidentiality of information about HIV-infected nurses must be maintained. Except in situations where a patient clearly has been exposed to an HIV-infected nurse's blood, the nurse should not be required to disclose his or her infection status.[48]

What is the likelihood of recovery of damages when a health care worker becomes HIV-positive as a result of occupational exposure?

Over 11,000 of the cases of HIV/AIDS reported in this country are among health care workers. Many exposures, however, go unreported because of fear of discrimination or loss of confidentiality,

The CDC has documented 40 cases of occupational transmission of HIV. Some of these individuals have initiated liability suits against their employers. Others have initiated suits for damages related to emotional distress from exposure to HIV. It would appear that in these cases, which are well documented by the CDC, individuals have encountered little difficulty obtaining workers' compensation benefits. It is uncertain how well individuals with less clearly documented cases may fare. There is now some question as to what type of wage and medical compensation benefits will be awarded in instances where health care workers cannot prove their infection occurred at the worksite.

Until recently, there was a "safety net" available to infected health care workers who could not prove work-relatedness or chose not to report. As a result of the U.S. Supreme Court's decision in *H & H Music Company*, employers now may cut the self-insurance benefits for workers with HIV or AIDS. The Equal Employment Opportunity Commission recently went to court to argue that such limitations are in violation of the ADA. The issue, however, has not yet been settled.

Some workers (e.g., firefighters and other emergency responders) have successfully sought to make chronic diseases, which have a higher relative risk in their occupations, a compensable condition through workers' compensation. Thus, the burden of proof has been shifted so that the employer is responsible for proving that the condition is not work-related. Benefits covering lost wages, medical expenses, disability, and death are therefore available to these workers. Nurses in several states have proposed and supported similar legislation regarding HIV and bloodborne infections.[49]

New workers' compensation provisions would require the introduction and passage of legislation on a state-by-state basis. Consideration is being given to the introduction of presumptive compensability legislation. Such legislation would, among other things, establish a presumption that a nurse or other health care worker who becomes HIV-positive after reporting a work-related exposure was infected on the job.

(Note: An HIV Task Force of the American Nurses Association has compiled for its state associations an extensive guide for the development of programs and materials designed to foster peer support for the HIV-positive nurse. Included in this material is information on disability coverage.)

Tuberculosis

Is there a specific standard governing exposure of health care workers to tuberculosis?

Data indicates that tuberculosis (TB) rates began to rise in 1984 and have increased steadily. In 1992, hospital administrators were warned of the possibility of potential fatalities among hospital workers and patients if a real commitment to TB control is not made in every U.S. hospital.[50]

In October 1994, the CDC issued guidelines for preventing the transmission of tuberculosis in health care facilities. The guidelines emphasize that early detection, isolation, and treatment of persons with active infectious TB are key in preventing the spread of the disease to health care workers. They prescribe the use of administrative controls and engineering controls according to the numbers of cases of TB encountered in the community, facility as a whole, and specific units of the facility. There also are detailed recommendations about TB testing and screening. One particular recommendation has met with considerable controversy—a call for workers who may be exposed to infectious TB to wear respirators equipped with high-efficiency particulate air (HEPA) filters.

The CDC is the leading agency for research and treatment guideline development. It can only make recommendations regarding the treatment of the public and workers. At this time, there is no specific standard governing the exposure of health care workers to tuberculosis. The Occupational Safety and Health Administration has resisted calls for an emergency temporary standard. Instead, OSHA issued a compliance memorandum to its regional offices providing guidance to inspectors in conducting TB-related inspections.

In the memorandum, OSHA emphasized that occupational exposure to TB is a serious and recognized hazard and certain feasible abatement methods exist and that the application of Section 5(a)(1) of the Occupational Safety and Health Act is warranted (commonly referred to as the "general duty clause"). The agency warned that failure to use any of the abatement methods listed in the memorandum "may result in the continued existence of a serious hazard and may, therefore, allow citation under 5(a)(1)." The five abatement methods are as follows:

1. Development of a protocol for early identification of individuals with active TB;

2. Medical surveillance, at no cost to employees, including replacement evaluation, administration, and interpretation of TB Mantoux skin tests, and periodic evaluations as indicated;

3. Evaluation and management, at no cost to employees, of workers with a positive skin test, or with skin test conversion on repeat testing, or who are exhibiting symptoms of TB;

4. Placement of individuals with suspected or confirmed TB in an acid-fast bacilli isolation room; and

5. Training and information to ensure that workers know the signs and symptoms of TB, medical surveillance and therapy, and site-specific protocols, including the proper use of controls.[51]

An OSHA standard governing exposure of health care workers to tuberculosis is expected in 1995. According to OSHA Administrator Joseph Dear, the standard "will very much take the CDC guidelines into account."[52]

(Also refer to ANA's brochure entitled *TB, a Deadly Disease Makes a Comeback,* which provides answers to questions commonly asked about tuberculosis.)

Ergonomics

Are there any measures to address ergonomic hazards?

Ergonomic hazards refer to a combination of stressors and/or workplace conditions that may cause harm to the worker. Improperly designed workstations, tools, and equipment; improper work methods; and excessive tool or equipment vibration are examples of this type of hazard. Other examples stem from job and process design problems that affect such factors as work flow, line speed, posture, force required, work/rest regimens, and repetition rates.

At this time, there is no ergonomic standard. However, employers have been cited for not providing a "safe and healthful workplace" as mandated by OSHA. In recent years, there has been a dramatic increase in the occurrence of cumulative trauma disorders (CTDs), or repetitive motion disorders, and other work-related injuries and illnesses due to ergonomic hazards. As a result, the number of penalties issued against companies for this type of safety and health violation has increased. Enforcement actions by OSHA have resulted in significant corporate-wide agreements requiring the implementation of comprehensive ergonomic programs. Currently, OSHA is working on a national standard and its release is imminent. It is anticipated that this standard will greatly affect the health care industry.

SUMMARY

Exercising employment rights and protections is basic to workplace survival. Given the complexity of state and federal legislation governing conditions of employment, it is important for nurses to understand basic workplace law and to stay apprised of legislative, legal, and agency activities having an impact on employment rights and protections.

3

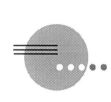

KNOW THE EMPLOYER AND TERMS AND CONDITIONS OF EMPLOYMENT

Health care has become a big business concerned with profits, efficiency, productivity, cost containment, quality, and competitive position in the industry.

CATHERINE D. BUCKLEY AND DIANE WALKER
Harmony: Professional Renewal for Nurses[53]

Nurses once employed by small, private health care institutions are suddenly finding themselves working for national chains or regional, multiunit systems. This may be only one of many changes in the employee-employer relationship. More employers are contracting with outside services to provide an entire management team or to oversee certain clinical services. Some employers are entering into arrangements in which two or more health care organizations share certain staff, services, and facilities.

As the health care industry takes on more of the trappings of corporate America, it is essential that nurses heighten their awareness of employment arrangements and potential terms and conditions of employment. A good starting point is to explore sources of information on employers, materials dealing with personnel policies and procedures, and strategies for dealing with special concerns.

EMPLOYMENT ARRANGEMENTS

What are the basic types of employment arrangements?

Employment relationships generally fall within one of four categories: employment-at-will, contractual agreements, lease arrangements, or self-employment (independent contractor). As noted in Chapter 2, the vast majority of employment relationships are entered into for an indefinite period of time. There either is no employment contract or the contract makes no mention of the job's duration. This arrangement is referred to as *employment-at-will.* (Also refer to the section "At-Will Employment" in Chapter 2.)

A second type of employment relationship is a contractual agreement. An individual employee or group of employees may enter into a written contract stating the terms of the employment relationship. One kind of written contract is a collective bargaining agreement, which is negotiated by the employer and a representative chosen by the employees. It is also possible that an employment contract may be entered into in a nonbargaining setting, either between individuals or a group of individuals.

A third type of employment relationship involves arrangements in which an individual enters into a relationship with a personnel organization which, in turn, arranges for the assignment of that individual to third parties (*lease arrangements*). Depending on the nature of the relationship, the personnel organization (e.g., brokerage, registry, or agency) may assume the legal obligations of an employer or treat its workers as independent contractors.

Independent contractor status is the fourth type of employment relationship. It refers to a self-employment arrangement in which an individual, among other things, exercises the right to direct and control his or her own work, operates separate and apart from the recipient of services, and takes financial risks.

The concept of independent contractor is explored more extensively in *Self-Employment in Nursing: Understanding the Basics of Starting a Business* published by American Nurses Publishing. The remainder of this chapter focuses on issues of special interest to individuals involved in at-will and contractual relationships.

EMPLOYER PROFILE

What should you know about your employer?

It is becoming increasingly important for nurses and other health care workers to be knowledgeable about an employer's: (1) values and priorities, (2) decision-making processes, (3) financial resources, and (4) short- and long-term plans. This type of information can be obtained from a variety of sources. The following are a few examples of readily accessible materials:

- *Mission statement*
  A mission statement is intended to be a reflection of an institution's primary objective, range of services, and ultimate goals. Information contained in a mission statement provides a general indication of how financial resources, staff, and facilities are being used and will continue to be used.

- *Organizational charts*
  A breakdown of the overall structure of operation may be particularly important when the employment setting is part of a national chain or multiunit system. By scrutinizing the "chain of command," it may be possible to determine where and how major decisions are actually made regarding the nature of services, personnel policies, management training, and marketing.

- *Annual reports*
  Annual reports usually contain information about the financial status of the institution, an overview of significant accomplishments and major activities,

and a listing of officers and directors. These reports frequently provide a concise delineation of both short- and long-term goals along with an indication of the institution's progress in achieving specific goals.

- ***In-house newsletters***
  Many employers routinely distribute an internal newsletter to apprise staff of new developments, matters requiring special attention, and staff recognition. By paying careful attention to these communications, it is often possible to identify emerging trends and issues.

- ***Promotional materials***
  Many health care providers prepare special newsletters for community distribution as well as general "public relations" brochures describing specific services and facilities. These items provide insight into the institution's marketing philosophy. How and to whom services are marketed have direct implications for the organization's financial viability.

- ***Media coverage***
  Local newspapers and business journals are likely to cover major developments or newsworthy events, such as merger activity, expansion of services, building plans, etc. Frequently, such reporting includes valuable background information about prior activities and future plans.

- ***Networking***
  Building relationships within the workplace can also be a valuable source of information. The cultivation of contacts in various units and departments can lead to a better understanding of the overall work environment.

In today's environment, it is particularly important to watch for any signs of changes in ownership, organization, or structuring. The need to strengthen market position has led many health care institutions to, among other things, engage in diversification, merger activity, corporate restructuring, and/or internal reorganization. (This type of activity is discussed at greater length in Chapter 4.)

PERSONNEL POLICIES

Where do you go to find specific information about personnel policies?

There are three primary sources of information regarding personnel policies in an employment setting: personnel policy manuals, employee handbooks, and collective bargaining agreements. According to the *Hospital Administration Handbook*,[54] personnel policies fall into six basic categories:

1. *Salary Programs and Economic Benefits*—policies on salary grades and ranges, shift premium pay, vacation leave, and insurance and other monetary benefits.

2. *Noneconomic Benefits and Employee Services*—policies on such provisions as employee health services, credit unions, arrangements for tax-deferred annuities, employee assistance programs, etc.

3. *Employee Relations Practices*—work rules and employee rights, including grievance and disciplinary procedures, meal and rest break provisions, and attendance/absenteeism policies.

4. *Major Noneconomic Personnel Programs*—policies on such provisions as performance appraisal, employee communication systems, employee training and development, retirement, etc.

5. *Management-Oriented Personnel Policies and Procedures*—direction regarding control over personnel utilization and expenses.

6. *Statements of Support and Compliance*—policies in areas such as Equal Employment Opportunity, Affirmative Action, and the Employee Retirement Income Security Act disclosure provisions.

Personnel Policy Manuals and Employee Handbooks

Personnel policy manuals and employee handbooks are the primary sources of information on employment policies. If nurses are covered under a collective bargaining agreement, the agreement supersedes any inconsistent personnel policy. If, however, the agreement is silent on certain subjects, the nurses are subject to/covered by the policies as set forth in the personnel policy manual.

All employers should have some sort of personnel policy manual. This document plays an important role in overall operations. It is a comprehensive resource on the policies, procedures, and activities within a given employment setting. Sections usually include specific information on employment classifications; orientation, transfer, and promotion policies; payroll, scheduling, and overtime practices; benefits; leaves of absence policies; performance, discipline, and grievance procedures; safety and security provisions; and layoff policies.

The personnel policy manual is used principally by administrators, managers, and supervisors. Each employee usually receives an abbreviated version in the form of an employee handbook. Nurses should be completely familiar with this document, as well as the contents of the entire manual. In most facilities, each unit is provided with a copy of the personnel policy manual.

Collective Bargaining Agreements

For nurses covered under a collective bargaining agreement, the contract outlines the terms and conditions of employment. Topics commonly covered include: employee status, work time, salary and related pay, fringe benefits (including pension provisions), discipline, grievance procedure, health and safety, nondiscrimination, in-service education, continuing education, leaves of absence, holidays, management rights, strikes and lockouts, layoffs, and termination. Many contracts also address professional issues. Contracts negotiated by state nurses associations, for example, may include language on the role of the nurse, non-nursing duties, staffing, professional practice committees, peer review, and tuition reimbursement. (A brochure is available from the American Nurses Association on how to organize a collective bargaining unit through the state nurses association.)

The major advantage of coverage under a collective bargaining agreement is the fact that it is a contract negotiated and signed by duly authorized representatives of management and nurses and is, therefore, binding and enforceable. Nurses in a bargaining unit should carefully study contract provisions and stay apprised of grievance settlements and any new interpretations of specific contract clauses. They also should be aware that personnel policy manuals and employee handbooks may provide rights or terms and conditions of employment not addressed in the bargaining agreement.

PERFORMANCE APPRAISAL

How do you determine the soundness of a performance appraisal system?

According to human resources experts, the performance appraisal process should serve both an evaluative and a developmental purpose. The evaluative dimension of appraisal generates data on past performance (ratings, rankings, field review, etc.). This information provides a base from which to make decisions regarding salary, promotion, transfer, or termination. The purpose is to improve performance by linking it closely to rewards. The developmental dimension of appraisal seeks to improve performance through self-learning and growth. The focus is on goal setting to broaden knowledge and expand skills.

Unfortunately, many appraisal systems fail to provide the necessary input/feedback to enhance employee performance. These systems may reflect all or many of the following weaknesses:

- The appraisal process is conducted by upper management rather than the employee's immediate supervisor.

- A single appraisal tool is used to evaluate all employees.

- Evaluation and assessment focuses on personal traits rather than work behavior.

- Behaviors which are the subject of evaluation/assessment fail to reflect the major substance of a specific job.

- The weighting of traits and behaviors does not reflect their significance in the performance of a specific job.

- Criteria for identifying an acceptable level of performance is vague, leaving it open to varying interpretations.

- There is little or no informal feedback on job performance, and formal evaluation occurs infrequently.[55]

When such characteristics are present, the appraisal process is apt to lack validity and/or reliability.

Performance appraisal is best handled at the management level closest to the employee. An immediate supervisor has firsthand knowledge of an employee's performance. An employee's job description should form the basis of any performance evaluation. A job description focuses on observable, measurable behaviors. It spells out precise job content, including duties, activities to be performed, responsibilities, and results expected by the employer. Ideally, a job description is developed in concert with an employee and his or her supervisor. Thus, both parties have a clear understanding of job expectations at the outset.

In writing about appraisal systems, Lynda Nauright notes that if the tasks included in a job description are specific, comprehensive, and are stated using action verbs, the base for a performance appraisal tool can be developed easily by adding a rating scale to the behaviors listed.[56] By using the job description as the foundation for performance evaluation, there is less likelihood that an employee will be evaluated on insignificant job behavior or personal traits.

To avoid any misunderstanding regarding the results of an appraisal, acceptable levels of performance must be clearly defined. If a rating scale is to be used, the meaning of each rating should be open to a single interpretation.

Finally, the appraisal system should allow for sufficient interaction throughout the process. Job performance appraisal should entail systematic assessment/evaluation throughout the designated period. Feedback (employment counseling, or "coaching") should be ongoing, including recommendations for improvement. As Barbara Stevens points out in *The Nurse as Executive*, the more frequent the evaluation of job performance, "the less stressful the situation becomes, and the more evaluation takes on the nature of guidance rather than . . . judgment."[57]

Employers have access to a variety of performance appraisal tools, ranging from checklists, ranking systems, and free-form essays, to management-by-objective methods and behaviorally anchored rating scales. A wide variety of factors influence the effectiveness of these and other tools. Consequently, it is not possible to offer a comprehensive discussion of the advantages and disadvantages associated with specific tools. Rather, the following questions are posed as one means of assessing the validity and reliability of an employer's appraisal system.

- Are employees actively involved in determining policies and procedures for the appraisal process?

- Is more than one type of performance appraisal tool used to evaluate an employee's performance? Are different tools used to evaluate different types of job assignments?

- Is job performance appraisal handled at the management level closest to the employee?

- Does the appraiser routinely collect relevant data about job performance, or depend on recall to meet a deadline for completing appraisal forms?

- Is there any type of review of a supervisor's appraisal of employees by upper management?

- Is there a standard time frame for formal evaluation (quarterly, biannually, annually, etc.)?

- Does the appraisal process include goal setting? Is there sufficient opportunity to review progress in achieving these goals during the appraisal period?

- Are the categories delineated in the evaluation tools realistic?

- Do the categories delineated in the evaluation tools complement the job description?

- Are the behaviors to be evaluated measurable?

- Do the formats of the appraisal tools provide space for recording supporting evidence/concrete illustrations?

- Are the standards/criteria for judging levels of job performance clearly defined?

- Do the evaluation tools weigh categories of employee behavior on the basis of their importance to the job?

- Is there clear understanding of the impact of performance appraisal on salary increments, job status, etc.?

- What recourse exists for an employee who is dissatisfied with the outcome of a job performance appraisal?

Responses to these questions provide insight into the overall effectiveness of a particular job performance appraisal system.

LIABILITY PROTECTION

What should a nurse know about workplace liability protection?

Claims experience indicates that nurse liability is a growing risk management issue. A study commissioned by the American Nurses Association (ANA) found that the average award in a claim against a nurse is $39,200.[58] Data from the Risk Management Foundation of the Harvard Medical Institutions reveal that, over the past 12 years, there has been an increase in the number of nurses named as sole defendants in health care malpractice suits. The most frequent allegations against nurses include (1) failure to ensure patient safety, (2) improper treatment or performance of treatment, (3) failure to monitor and to report, (4) medication errors and reactions, and (5) failure to follow hospital procedure.

Over the past few years, a number of states have updated laws regulating nursing practice—increasing the instances in which nurses are legally accountable for exercising judgment independent of the physician. With this expanding responsibility comes increased liability. Consequently, it is important for nurses to investigate the nature of their employer's liability coverage—the amount of coverage, whether it is a *claims-made* or an *occurrence* policy, and whether it includes professional liability or only malpractice coverage. This information should be obtained in writing. An attorney should check over the information for any loopholes that could leave an employee vulnerable in the event of a lawsuit.

Most health care facilities carry "claims-made" insurance. Thus, if a nurse is no longer working at the insured facility or the facility closes, the nurse is not covered when a claim is filed. Moreover, an employer's policy only covers the nurse within the confines of the work setting. If a nurse gives advice to a friend or renders care to someone in an emergency outside of work, the employer's policy is not in effect. For these and other reasons, the ANA recommends that every practicing registered nurse should carry his or her own professional liability insurance coverage. ANA, state nurses associations, and other national nursing organizations have developed materials for nurses explaining how to obtain adequate insurance protection, what to do in the event of the threat of a lawsuit, and how to prevent nursing malpractice.

To assess the potential for liability problems in a given employment setting, consider the following key questions:

- Does an effective system exist for identifying problem situations?

- Is there a process for screening and determining the seriousness of each problem?

- Do review, analysis, and resolution take place as part of the system?

- Do follow-up procedures correct or eliminate incident/accident causes?

- Does factual, comprehensive documentation exist in most risk situations?

- Are appropriate means established and understood by staff for reporting problems (incidents and accidents)?

- Does adequate documentation occur when a problem is identified?

- Are comprehensive polices and procedures relative to the handling of incidents and accidents formulated and followed?

- Do these policies and procedures incorporate definitions of responsibility and authority?

- Does the employer have a systematic method of centrally recording and maintaining incidents and accidents?

- Does the employer's attorney receive copies of all major incident/accident reports and support information?

- Are good investigative techniques and judgments used to determine the best course of action in the resolution of problems?

- Are general problems—in terms of trends and patterns—identified, addressed, and resolved?[59]

The responses to these and related questions provide the basis from which to assess an employer's defense against possible litigation.

FAMILY-ORIENTED POLICIES AND BENEFITS

Does an employer have any obligation to assist employees in dealing with family-oriented problems?

In 1990, the Conference Board encouraged employers to give greater attention to the life-cycle stages of their employees in tailoring special benefits. According to the Conference Board, a life-cycle approach to family benefits and policies takes into account the following stages: new worker, marriage, pregnancy and adoption, childrearing, divorce, eldercare, retirement, and death.[60]

The Women's Bureau of the U.S. Department of Labor (DOL) has compiled a work and family resource kit to assist employers "in balancing the conflicting and competing demands of work and family life."[61] The purpose of the kit is to help employers understand the range of family needs emerging in the workplace and the potential options for employer response. According to the Women's Bureau, family-oriented policies and benefits fall into three broad categories: (1) dependent care options; (2) alternative work schedules; and (3) benefits, leaves, and services.[62]

Dependent Care Options

Since 1980, there has been dramatic growth in the portion of the workforce needing child care services in order to work. Today, a majority of employers provide some form of child care support for their employees. Assistance to working parents takes a variety of forms, including the following:

- Resource and referral programs to provide employees with information, ranging from lists of day care centers to assistance in evaluating and choosing a child care provider;

- Child care home networks—coordinated systems of licensed family-home child care centers managed by the employer or outside agency;

- Babysitting training to improve the quality of child care available in the community;

- Employer-operated day care centers on the employment premises or offsite;

- Vendor discounts—an employer contracts with an independent day care center to provide a number of slots for employees' children at a reduced rate;

- Voucher programs—an employer offers a cash benefit directly to employees to be spent on child care of the parent's choosing;

- Emergency/sick child care services through hospital sick bay services or community agencies providing in-home care; and

- School-age child care before and after school and during vacations.

As the elderly population expands, the issue of "eldercare" is also becoming more prominent. The U.S. Department of Labor (DOL) estimates that 25 to 30% of the workforce will eventually face caregiving responsibilities for aging relatives.[63] According to DOL, employers have begun to observe the negative effects on work performance caused by eldercare responsibilities and are responding with information, financial assistance for employees, and contributions to local programs.[64] Some employers, for example, provide information about the array of services for the elderly through seminars, support groups, handbooks, hotlines, and employee assistance programs. A few employers have begun providing reimbursement or direct subsidies to employees for visiting nurse costs, making it easier for employees to go to work when medical needs arise among elderly dependents. Others are examining new health insurance options to help employees pay for long-term care for themselves or dependent children, spouses, or parents.

Alternative Work Schedules

To help working parents, some employers have initiated various work schedule options, such as compressed work weeks, job sharing, permanent and temporary part-time employment, and voluntary reduced work time programs. According to the American Management Association, the proven benefits of flexible scheduling include improvement in quality of work, decreased tardiness, and a greater level of job satisfaction.[65]

"Flextime" was initiated by the federal government on an experimental basis in 1979 and was made a permanent feature of employment for federal workers in 1985. Today, more than 500,000 federal employees and over 10 million private sector workers are involved in flexible and compressed work schedule programs.[66]

Within health care settings, flextime has been accomplished by providing variable prescheduled shift start times, shift lengths, and percentages of work.[67] However, with growing attention focusing on restructuring measures (including job redesign), the issue of work schedules is receiving closer scrutiny in many facilities.

Benefits, Leaves, and Services

Studies indicate that more employers are creating fringe benefits and services to better address family-related needs and concerns. One popular approach is to offer flexible benefit or cafeteria plans—allowing employees to choose from a range of benefits that suit individual needs.[68] A typical flexible benefit plan provides several core benefits, including basic medical coverage. In addition, a number of optional benefits are made available, including such provisions as child care services, educational assistance, physical fitness programs, additional vacation time, life insurance, dental insurance, and legal aid.

Telephone access and time off to deal with family emergencies are among the topics covered in many family-oriented policies. Growing attention is being given to leave that allows either parent to spend a designated period of time with a newborn or newly adopted child and then return to work, assuming the same position. (Also refer to the section "Family and Medical Leave" in Chapter 2.) More employers are making allowances for time off each year to enable working parents to make needed medical appointments, participate in parent-teacher conferences, or attend special school activities. Some employers have also created policies allowing employees to maintain contact with their children or babysitters during the work day. Rather than limiting family interaction by telephone to emergencies, working parents are able to deal routinely with family concerns.

Employee assistance programs (EAPs) are also being viewed as appropriate channels for dealing with the stress associated with conflicts between home and work responsibilities. Studies indicate that, over the past few years, family/marital problems have accounted for as much as 35% of EAP caseloads.[69]

It also is worth noting that the International Foundation of Employee Benefit Plans predicts that by the year 2000, the workforce will be offered a greater range of nontraditional benefits. These benefits, according to the foundation, are likely to cover a range of opportunities, including financial planning, long-term care insurance, retraining, sex/minority sensitivity workshops, family counseling, and mentor/career counseling.[70]

Every nurse needs to make an accurate assessment of how family responsibilities may influence job performance. It is then important to determine how existing personnel policies and employer-sponsored benefits and services address family-related issues. By staying apprised of the trends, nurses are in a better position to seek an expansion of policies and fringe benefits to better meet their needs and the needs of other workers.

LAYOFF PROVISIONS

In the event of layoffs, what type of severance package can an employee expect?

Job security is a growing concern for people in all industries. Reports of "workforce reductions" have become commonplace. On a weekly basis, the media covers downsizing, retooling, and restructuring of workforces in various segments of industry and major business. Reasons for such activities range from efforts to reduce expenses and increase profits to measures designed to reduce bureaucracy or avoid a hostile takeover.

The type of employer assistance made available to laid-off employees often depends on the amount of planning that goes into the layoff decision. If workforce reduction is handled in an uncontrolled fashion (e.g., rapid layoffs of large groups of personnel), there is apt to be little, if any, warning of impending layoffs and minimal provisions for assisting employees in making the transition into the general workforce. On the other hand, when downsizing is strategically planned, there is apt to be careful consideration about how best to assist affected employees.

Some downsizing techniques, being used in all industries, are intended to provide some stability for the employee and the organization and to allow for planned transition in the workforce. These techniques include the following:

- Early retirement offers to selected employee groups;
- Voluntary layoff buyout packages that provide severance pay and outplacement services;
- Cutbacks in salary, hourly pay, and/or overtime;
- Cutbacks in work hours;
- Reduction of positions through attrition;
- Outplacement services and job banks instituted in advance of layoffs; and
- Career planning services.

Since 1993, there has been a significant increase in layoffs within the health care industry, particularly in hospitals. Information collected by the American Nurses Association points to two reasons for reductions in full-time equivalent (FTE) registered nurse (RN) positions: workplace restructuring and economics. According to ANA, workplace restructuring often involves cross-training, substitution, and/or work elimination. Low census numbers and cost-containment efforts are cited among the economic factors contributing to a reduction in RN positions.[71]

Alarmed by the growing number of reports of nurse layoffs, ANA has made "job security and the protection of hospital-based RN positions from inappropriate substitution of lesser-skilled personnel" high priorities of the association.[72] ANA advocates that all laid-off employees should be given a severance package and outplacement services.

Severance is compensation that the employer chooses to pay on termination beyond what the employee is entitled to as payment for wages, vacation, sick time, or other benefits. Severance pay acknowledges that an employee has been "severed" from the organization. It is also intended to recognize a subsequent period of unemployment. The purpose of outplacement services is to help an employee cope with the abrupt termination of employment and find another position. Outplacement services typically include: general counseling, career counseling, job advice, retraining and skill classes, resume development, coaching in interview techniques, and job placement assistance.[73]

Any agreements regarding severance pay and outplacement services should be in writing. An employee also should be entitled to information regarding the formula used to calculate severance pay. In most cases, before an employer releases the severance check, an employee will be asked to sign a document relinquishing any rights to take legal action against the employer as a result of being laid off.

ANA encourages nurses who are facing layoff to seek answers to a number of questions, including the following:

Severance Pay

- What formula was used to determine the pay?

- How are the years of employment determined?

- How does the formula account for part-time or per diem work and leaves of absences?

- At what rate will severance be taxed?

- Will severance be paid in a lump sum or installments?

- Will severance pay affect the right to be recalled?

Outplacement Services

- What services are included in the outplacement package?

- How long are the services being offered?

- Are they being offered as an addition to severance pay or as an alternative to severance pay?

- Are there different outplacement packages being offered and what criteria were utilized to determine which employee groups receive which package?[74]

It must be emphasized that receipt of a severance package or outplacement services is not an exchange for unemployment benefits. All paperwork should clearly indicate that the action reflects the employer's decision and is "an involuntary release from work" and, therefore, entitles the individual to unemployment benefits.

(Also refer to the section "Layoffs" in Chapter 2 for a discussion of legislative provisions regarding layoffs.)

GRIEVANCE HANDLING

What are the components of a valid grievance process?

A grievance procedure, no matter whether it is a contractual provision or employer-initiated, must meet certain criteria to effectively resolve workplace problems. The ideal grievance procedure assures that an employee's complaint is handled fairly, quickly, and without fear of reprisal. The essential components should:

1. Provide for consideration of all complaints, disputes, or differences, so that important problems are not ruled out due to technicalities.

2. Provide for simple steps and time limits, as this encourages the fixing of responsibility and results in prompt settlement at the lowest possible level.

3. Provide for employee representation at each step so that complaints are presented properly and are assured of a fair hearing.

4. Provide for ultimate decision making by an objective and impartial third party, or, at the very least, examination/review by an independent, neutral party.[75]

A key element in a fair grievance procedure is the orderly series of steps, progressing upward through successively higher levels of administration and ending in binding arbitration. Time schedules for handling grievances may differ, but the ultimate objective is to expedite the grievance as quickly as possible. No matter what the circumstances, there are certain facts and guidelines about grievance handling that every nurse should know.

Categories of Grievances

A grievance may stem from any situation that is outside a nurse's control. It may involve one nurse, several nurses, all nurses in the unit, or other employees. Generally, grievances fall into five categories:

1. A grievance may arise from management's infraction of a contract.

2. A grievance may arise from management's infraction of federal, state, or local laws relating to conditions of employment.

3. A grievance may arise from management's disregard of past practices related to contractual terms and conditions of employment.

4. A grievance may arise from a failure of management to meet its responsibilities (i.e., disregard for the health and safety of employees).

5. A grievance may arise from management's violation of its own rules or policies.

Written Complaint

It is important that the grievant put the complaint in writing as quickly as possible. A written grievance should contain: (1) the facts of the grievance in clear, concise terms; (2) the contract provision, rule, or practice that has been violated; and (3) the specific remedy or proposed disposition being sought.

In writing out the complaint and preparing the presentation, it is important to distinguish between fact and opinion in the selection of information. It is also important to determine which facts are most relevant to the matter under consideration. Clear and concise answers should be developed for the following questions:

- What happened?
- When did it occur?
- Where did it occur?
- Who was involved?
- Were there any witnesses?
- Why is this a grievance?
- What other factual information may be needed?
- What must management do to correct this problem?

Grievance Presentation

The grievance process may involve several levels of appeal. In making a grievance presentation before an immediate supervisor, director of nursing, administrator, or impartial third party (arbitrator), certain guidelines should be followed:

- Stick to the issues.
- Be factual in presenting information.

- Listen to the other side—What is the underlying reason for their position? What are the weaknesses in that position?

- Make an effort to save face for both sides—nothing is gained through a bad relationship.

- Summarize the discussion at the end of the meeting to be sure that all parties have the same understanding.

- Write minutes and a summary of the meeting in detail for future reference.

- Do not make threats.

- Do not make "deals"—one nurse's grievance should not be resolved at the expense of another nurse.

Nurses covered by a collective bargaining agreement will have access to a bargaining unit representative whose primary responsibility is grievance handling. This individual will assess the validity of the grievance, help put the complaint in writing, gather the essential information, and assist with the presentation of the grievance throughout the process.

SPECIAL CONSIDERATIONS

Given the growing complexity of health care and the many changes occurring within the industry, nurses and other health care workers face a growing number of legal and ethical dilemmas. The nature of the work environment and the type of support and assistance offered by the employer greatly affect how these challenges are addressed.

Illegal, Unethical, and Incompetent Practices

Should an employer provide a mechanism for reporting illegal, unethical, and incompetent practices?

Nurses have a professional obligation to report illegal, unethical, and incompetent practices. Incompetent nursing practice is measured by nursing standards; unethical practice is evaluated in light of the Code for Nurses; and illegal practice is identified in terms of violation of the law.[76]

According to the American Nurses Association, "each employing institution/ agency providing nursing services has an obligation to establish a process for the reporting and handling of practices by individual or by health care systems that jeopardize client health or safety."[77] The association has identified a number of nonlegal strategies that employers and employees may use to protect and encourage reporting activities. These strategies include:

- More than one internal channel for communicating complaints and comments;

- An internal process for employees to seek informal clarification of institutional policies and laws;

- Assurances of a workplace free of any reprisals for responsible reporting;

- An "open door" policy, allowing employees to take complaints through all the chains of command; and

- A formal grievance and arbitration procedure.[78]

Implementation of these and similar strategies are intended to encourage employees to take their concerns to the employer, rather than outside sources. However, it also should be noted that employees who decide to report employer violations of the law to appropriate outside agencies may be accorded certain rights and protections under the laws governing whistleblowing. (Refer to the section "Whistleblowing" in Chapter 2.)

Assignment Despite Objection

What recourse is available when an assignment is unacceptable?

Since the early 1980s, a growing number of nurses have voiced concerns about their right to accept or reject a staffing assignment. Because of the uniqueness of individual state practice acts, other state statutes governing employment, and judicial and administrative decisions, it would be impossible to devise a standard set of guidelines to apply to every potential situation. It also would be difficult, if not inappropriate, to generalize about decisions made in various settings under differing circumstances.

It must be emphasized that the decision to accept or reject an assignment includes the real likelihood of discipline by the employer. However, acceptance of an assignment need not be without question. Nurse attorney Maureen Cushing, for example, offers the following advice on how to challenge an assignment:

- Carefully evaluate the reasons for challenging an assignment (e.g., Is the assignment an unreasonable demand?);

- Thoroughly discuss the assignment with the supervisor (e.g., acknowledge limitations, clarify the assignment, ask questions about the setting and reasons for assignment);

- Identify possible options or alternatives for assignments (e.g., sharing the assignment among several nurses, calling in a qualified off-duty nurse, trading assignments with a qualified nurse from another unit); and

- Document the situation, using a form specifically designed for such purposes.[79]

For many years, the American Nurses Association has supported the use of assignment-despite-objection (ADO) forms to document unexpected or inadequate staffing. A number of state nurses associations (SNAs), in consultation with legal counsel, have developed such tools. One state association, for example, developed a specific form for documenting questionable practice situations. The SNA encourages nurses to use the form when an assignment exceeds the limits of the nurse's educational preparation and clinical expertise, when patient volume makes the assignment unsafe, or when an assignment goes beyond the legal scope of nursing practice. While the filing of such a document cannot absolve a nurse from all liability, it does "shift the responsibility of the unsafe assignment back onto the hospital or agency and the assigning supervisor."[80]

SUMMARY

Knowing about the employer and the terms and conditions of employment involves careful scrutiny of a variety of factors. The short- and long-range plans of the employer, the nature and scope of personnel policies, the type of performance appraisal, the availability of special fringe benefits and provisions for layoffs, the process for grievance handling, and other special considerations influence the overall work environment. These and other factors can either facilitate or impede a nurse's ability to function effectively. Consequently, knowledge of the employer and employment conditions, coupled with an understanding of workplace law, forms the foundation on which to cultivate workplace survival skills.

4

UNDERSTAND THE WORK ENVIRONMENT

Today's nurse practices in an environment which is vastly more complicated culturally, technologically, and bureaucratically than any of her nursing sisters of the past, even the very recent past, have known.

CATHERINE MURPHY AND HOWARD HUNTER
Ethical Problems in the Nurse-Patient Relationship[81]

Within the span of a very few years, the health care industry has changed dramatically—creating a work environment for nurses that is far more complex and challenging. Facilities are restructuring, systems are being streamlined, and jobs are being redesigned. At the same time, new and different types of workplace issues are emerging. To function effectively, nurses must develop the ability to interpret and act upon a myriad of signals. This chapter looks at several specific areas of concerns, reflecting the broad range of factors influencing today's work environment.

RESTRUCTURING

The ownership, organization, and structure of all health care institutions are coming under close scrutiny. Some restructuring efforts have been justified and carefully planned. Many measures, however, appear to be "quick fixes" that fail to take into account the long-range implications for both consumers and health care workers.

What type of restructuring is occurring in the health care industry?

Within the health care industry, restructuring commonly involves business reorganization and/or work redesign. The greatest amount of activity has been concentrated within hospital and acute care settings. According to one source, restructuring is occurring "in every geographic area, in every type and size of hospital."[82]

Business (corporate) reorganization involves such activities as mergers and acquisitions, diversification, and/or innovative partnerships. According to data compiled by the American Hospital Association, approximately 195 mergers and con-solidations involving 404 hospitals occurred between 1980 and 1991. More than 50% of this activity took place after 1986. According to industry analysts, the increase in hospital mergers during the latter part of the 1980s was triggered, in part, by the shift in health care delivery from inpatient to outpatient settings. In addition, Medicare's prospective payment system, which led to dwindling margins, and the growth in managed care are said to have fueled merger activity.

In addition, some institutions have chosen to diversify, forming systems that also own businesses which interface with provider facilities (e.g., suppliers of surgical equipment). These arrangements vary in size from the combination of two facilities to the corporate ownership of hundreds of facilities and services. They may be multiunit systems limited to a specific geographic area or national and international chains.

Large and small, formal and informal partnerships between hospitals, local gov-ernment, business, and community organizations also are emerging. According to the president of the American Hospital Association, the industry has come to realize that there is no future in competing for "the biggest piece of an increasingly shrink-ing pie."[83] As a result, greater emphasis is being placed on collaborative efforts.

These and other activities have resulted in a variety of structural configurations, including group purchasing arrangements, service consolidation, physician sharing, physician practice arrangements with hospitals, sharing of professional education and development resources, vertical integration of previously separate entities, buy-out with continued operation of separate facilities, and corporate merger with full integration of workforce and services. In some instances, changes have had little or no impact on the individual entities. In other instances, they have necessitated reassignment of personnel due to facility or unit closures, layoffs due to service consolidation, relocation of staff development programs, introduction of new man-agement and other personnel, transfer of personnel to a different facility, and/or greater reliance on contract services.

For several years, the American Nurses Association (ANA) has been tracking hospital mergers, acquisitions, and closures in an effort to provide nurses with information about what to look for in a hospital setting that might indicate impend-ing reorganization or closure. According to the association, early warning signs include:

- Census consistently less than 50% of staffed beds.

- Declining operating margins for the past 2 to 3 years.

- Visibly aging facility with poor geographic access.

- Large numbers of Medicare and Medicaid patients.

- High levels of uncompensated care.

- Few managed care contracts.

- High labor costs, regardless of mix.

- High levels of debt.

- Open conflict between administrators, physicians, and governing board.

- Open disputes with community groups.

- Presence of consultants.

- Sudden revision of acuity system.

- Unexpected midcycle budget review.[84]

Nurses who suspect their facility may be planning to merge, be acquired, or close are encouraged to contact their state nurses association for information on how to respond to such activity.

Restructuring also takes the form of redesigning work and staffing configurations. According to one group of researchers, *work redesign* is "widespread" in hospitals across the country.[85] It would appear that the overriding goal of most work redesign efforts is to cut costs. Because nurses are the largest employee group in hospitals, they are a primary target for redesign measures. Many hospitals have increased registered nurses' work responsibilities and simultaneously increased their substitution with lesser skilled workers.

Based on information gathered by the American Nurses Association, a plan of work redesign is likely to include some combination of the following:

- Consolidation of management services and reduction in management layers through management layoffs, reducing labor costs, and streamlining the organization.

- Early retirement programs and buy-out for staff with seniority.

- Implementation of nursing care models that change the nursing skill mix, lowering labor costs by replacing more costly registered nurses (RNs) with lesser-skilled and lower-paid ancillary staff.

- Reassignment of RNs or reduction in force.

- Substitution of RNs by paramedical staff, replacing RN full-time equivalents (FTEs) with lesser-paid employees.

- Increased use of licensed practical nurses (LPNs), further decreasing the number of RN FTEs and increasing the RN's role of responsibility.

- Cross-training of RNs to other nursing specialties.

- Cross-training of RNs to non-nursing clinical tasks.

- Cross-training of ancillary staff.

- An increase in part-time positions and a corresponding decrease in full-time positions.

- Elimination of preferential staffing and scheduling systems.

- Reduced hours of operation for ancillary departments with a corresponding shift to the nursing units.[86]

Significant issues have been raised regarding work redesign plans. These issues focus on potentially unsafe staffing levels, inappropriate use of assistive personnel and aides, and potential or actual layoffs.

There is growing evidence that the inappropriate substitution of other personnel for registered nurses will lead to deterioration in the quality and safety of health care. Research has documented a statistically significant relationship between the level and mix of nursing staff in hospitals and patient outcomes. Changes in nurse staffing levels and skill mix must be justified in terms of both their cost and effect on important patient care outcomes, such as mortality, length of stay, patient satisfaction, and adverse occurrences.

It is extremely important that nurses lead workplace redesign efforts. They must become actively involved in hospital committees that collect patient outcome data. They need to identify workplace committees that influence quality and resource distribution and seek appointment of nurses to these groups or target key members to influence.

Nursing groups and others have raised strong concerns regarding any restructuring plans that decrease the use of registered nurses and increase the use of lower-paid assistive personnel. To this end, ANA has prepared a special brochure entitled *Every Patient Deserves a Nurse*, which contains a checklist for consumers to assess the quality of nursing care in hospitals.

Finally, there appears to be yet another dimension of restructuring activity on the horizon, which involves the concept of *reengineering*. According to Michael Hammer, reengineering is defined as the "fundamental rethinking and radical redesign of business processes to achieve dramatic improvements in contemporary measures of performance, such as cost, quality, service, and speed."[87]

When applied to health care organizations, one consultant defines reengineering as "the radical redesign of the critical systems and processes used to produce, deliver, and support patient care in order to achieve dramatic improvements in organizational performance within a short-period of time."[88] Because it is "an idea just beginning to emerge in health care," experts agree that it is too early to judge its outcome.[89]

Clearly, nurses need to be alert to signals of impending changes in their work environments. They need to be involved in the decision-making process and to carefully monitor changes as they are occurring. Every employee affected by restructuring should have a voice in deciding how restructuring efforts will be carried out.

Learning to ask the right questions is critical. Key considerations include the process used to make major decisions, the exact nature of the changes, the rationale for initiating the changes, the timetable for implementation, and the projected impact. Equally important is the determination of a means for evaluating the effectiveness of changes. In the initial planning stages, criteria should be developed for measuring the level of success of specific measures and a plan of action devised for addressing problems.

CONTINUOUS IMPROVEMENT CULTURE

Quality controls are another major factor affecting the workplace. In the late 1970s and early 1980s, many health care institutions began relying more heavily upon utilization review to ensure quality while containing costs. During this same period, quality assurance programs grew in popularity as an effective means of identifying problems associated with single events or single settings. Over time, these programs expanded to focus on entire patient care episodes and to better recognize the relationship between the system and provider in affecting quality outcomes.[90]

By the mid-1980s, increasing competition among hospitals and the need to become more cost-efficient prompted many hospital chief executive officers to explore the possibility of designing new systems to measure and to manage the quality of services in a given facility. This exercise led health care experts to study the application of industrial quality control techniques.

Most health care organizations now have quality assurance and risk management systems. Many even have unit-based quality assurance for specific key indicators. This fact prompted many experts to reason that the major elements of quality control were already in place within the health care industry and that the next logical step was to institute total quality management and continuous quality improvement (TQM/CQI).

What are the characteristics of successful quality management?

The implementation of TQM/CQI has necessitated fundamental changes in work methods. Decentralization, emphasis on interdisciplinary collaboration, changes in skill mix, and various attempts at work redesign (e.g., patient-centered care) are closely linked to quality initiatives within the health care industry. Unfortunately, there is considerable debate regarding the effectiveness of these and other measures. As Jacqueline Dienemann points out: "Quality enhancement is the watchword in health care today, yet researchers find a minority of continuous quality improvement programs are successful."[91]

According to several sources, few organizations have successfully shifted their values, energies, and resources to properly implement the TQM philosophy.[92] Instead, employers use elements of TQM/CQI theory as smokescreens for enhancing economic position and increasing profits. In the process, the quality of patient care actually suffers as budgets are cut, staffs reduced, and employees excluded from decision-making processes. Given this fact, it is crucial for nurses to understand the fundamental principles of effective quality improvement programs.

TQM embodies three key ingredients: participative management, continuous process improvement, and the use of teams.[93] The basic objective is to involve employees in the analysis of their daily work processes in an effort to stimulate innovation and productivity. The ultimate goal is the improvement of service to "customers." The following key words and concepts are reflective of the basic principles associated with TQM/CQI: (1) customer focus, (2) focus on process as well as results, (3) prevention versus inspection, (4) mobilizing the expertise of the workforce, (5) fact-based decision making, and (6) feedback.[94]

Certain groundwork must be laid to foster a work environment supportive of valid quality management practices. According to experts, a sound foundation for supporting TQM/CQI includes the following characteristics:

- Every level of the organization is committed to quality management and fully involved.

- The values of the organization demonstrate a shift from strictly financial outcomes to patient outcomes.

- There is a shift from centralized control to empowerment of front-line personnel.

- Training in quality management and improvement is provided at all levels of the organization.

- Managers relinquish responsibility for controlling and/or directing employees in favor of facilitation and coordination.

- Every member of an interdisciplinary team is viewed as a full partner.

- Decision making is based on all available data.

- Both horizontal and vertical communication is continuous and free-flowing.

- Tools are in place to allow for periodic review of quality controls.

- Recognition and incentive programs are in place throughout the organization to reward quality improvements.

- Educational support is routinely offered in such areas as communication, group dynamics, assertiveness, delegation skills, and change management.

By far, the most significant shortcoming of many TQM/CQI programs in health care settings is the failure to solicit the participation of front-line workers, especially nurses, in decision making. Styles of management/leadership as well and decision-making processes are key elements in successful quality management programs. Both of these topics are discussed more extensively in Chapter 5.

WORKFORCE DIVERSITY

What are the implications of a more diverse workforce?

One of the most significant characteristics associated with the workforce of the 1990s and beyond is "diversity"—diversity in terms of gender, color, nationality, and culture. Data compiled by the Department of Labor indicates that, by the year 2000, 42.8 million people will have joined the U.S. workforce. Approximately 68% of these individuals will be American-born women, blacks, Hispanics, Asians, Native Americans, and other groups. According to one source, these individuals—with their diverse cultures and backgrounds—will bring "different perceptions, different value systems, and different languages to the workplace."[95]

The changing demographics of workers have become readily apparent in the health care industry. For example, one hospital directory identifies the names of employees from 40 different countries who would be willing to translate for patients. Foreign-born and foreign-educated physicians now represent almost 20% of physicians licensed in the United States. Clinical professionals trained in their home countries now occupy a significant share of technical and laboratory positions in the nation's hospitals.[96]

Recently, growing emphasis has been placed on the impact of cultural differences on health beliefs and practices. Much less attention, however, has focused on the implications for workplace dynamics. As one nurse educator points out, "In the nonpatient relationship, nurses pay little attention to cultural beliefs and how these diverse beliefs affect the work setting."[97] In an article on teaching cultural diversity for the workplace, Christine Lajkowicz suggests that there is a tendency on the part of nurses to assume that all staff members have the same beliefs.[98] According to Lajkowicz, "this approach can impede the attainment of work-related goals and professional growth."[99]

Within the work environment, it is extremely important to recognize that culture does influence what workers perceive to be appropriate or acceptable behavior and how they communicate or expect others to communicate.[100] Mildred Roberson suggests: "In order to be effective, both in providing nursing care and interacting with co-workers . . . nurses must gain sufficient knowledge and skills to develop a *transcultural perspective.*"[101]

While it would be impossible to be familiar with all cultural beliefs and values, it is crucial for nurses and other health care workers to achieve greater "cultural sensitivity."[102] An important first step is to develop an understanding of one's own culture and how it has an impact on behavior. The next step is to learn more about the specific beliefs, values, and practices of co-workers.

Communication plays a key role in managing diversity—minimizing any tensions resulting from race, gender, or culture-based differences among workers. Communication experts recommend paying closer attention to language and expression, affect, posture, gestures, body movements, and use of personal space.[103] Choice of words can be extremely important. The same words may mean different things to people because of cultural differences. The interpretation of body language (e.g., gestures, eye contact, handshake, or facial expressions) also varies according to culture. In certain cultures, for example, people may be taught to avoid eye contact. Sensitivity to these and other nuances will become increasingly important.

SEXUAL HARASSMENT

Sexual harassment in the workplace is a relatively contemporary issue. The first studies on the subject were conducted approximately 20 years ago by the Working Women's Institute.

As indicated in Chapter 2, unwelcome sexual advances, requests for sexual favors, and other verbal or physical conduct of a sexual nature constitutes sexual harassment under the following circumstances:

1. Submission is made either explicitly or implicitly a term or condition of an individual's employment;

2. Submission to or rejection of such conduct is used as the basis for employment decisions affecting an individual; or

3. Such conduct has the purpose or effect of unreasonably interfering with an individual's work performance or creating an intimidating, hostile, or offensive work environment.

Sexual harassment can occur in a variety of circumstances. The victim, as well as the harasser, may be a man or a woman. The victim does not have to be of the opposite sex of the harasser. The harasser may be the victim's supervisor, a co-worker, or a nonemployee.

Sexual harassment usually falls into one of three categories:

Verbal: sexual innuendo, suggestive comments, threats, insults, jokes about gender-specific traits, sexual propositions;

Nonverbal: making suggestive or insulting noises, obscene gestures, whistling, leering; or

Physical: touching, pinching, brushing body, coercing sexual intercourse, assault.[104]

How prevalent is sexual harassment in nursing?

Although much has been written on sexual harassment in business and industry, there is little documentation on sexual harassment in nursing. However, available data suggest that a significant percentage of nurses are victims of sexual harassment. In light of this fact, the American Nurses Association issued a position statement on sexual harassment in 1993. Acknowledging that nurses and nursing students have a right to a workplace free of sexual harassment, the association emphasized the following:

- Preventive measures must be established. Employers of nurses must recognize the magnitude of the problem and establish policies and procedures that protect individuals from sexual harassment.

- Educational programs should be offered that define sexual harassment and communicate the institution's position, policy, and procedure for reporting.

- Top level management and boards must demonstrate their commitment not only through verbal and written communications, but through their actions.

- Every nursing employer and school of nursing should have a written policy statement on sexual harassment. Every employee and nursing student should be oriented to this policy at the time of employment or enrollment.

- The policy statement should include the purpose, legal definition and guidelines, employee and management responsibilities, implementation procedure, grievance procedure, nonretaliation statement, and disciplinary measures for employees and nonemployees. The policy statement should also specify how confidentiality will be ensured.[105]

According to ANA, if a written policy does not currently exist or the above elements are not included, an interdisciplinary committee should be convened to establish one. In those settings in which nurses are represented through a collective bargaining agreement, language should be incorporated into the contract that remedies sexual harassment complaints through grievance and arbitration procedures.[106]

In settings in which a sexual harassment policy is in place, nurses are encouraged to consider the following questions:

Policy Considerations

- Has the employer made all employees fully aware of its policy and procedures dealing with sexual harassment?
- Does the employer's policy make it clear that sexual harassment investigations will be conducted on a confidential basis?
- Does the employer hold routine training programs for supervisors, managers, and employees on sexual harassment?

Investigating Process

- Who conducts the investigation?
- Who is interviewed during the investigative process?
- To whom are the results of the investigation communicated?

Remedies

- Are complaints of sexual harassment acted upon immediately and investigated fully?
- How are violators disciplined?
- What factors influence the type of discipline that is administered?[107]

Nurses and others who experience sexual harassment in the workplace are encouraged to use the following strategies:

1. **Confront** the harasser, repeatedly if necessary, and clearly ask that the harassment stop.
2. **Report** the harassment to authorities, using the "chain of command" in the organization and whatever formal complaint channels are available.
3. **Document** the harassment, writing down the who, what, where, and when and keeping as detailed a record as possible.
4. **Seek** support from others, such as colleagues or an organized group.[108]

(For additional information refer to ANA's brochure on *Sexual Harassment, It's Against the Law.*)

WORKPLACE VIOLENCE

Is violence in health care settings on the increase?

Over the past few years, issues of safety have become a growing concern among health care workers in every setting in all parts of the country (i.e., urban, inner city, and rural areas). Data published by the *Journal of Healthcare Protection Management*, for example, document incidents of sexual assault, arson, battery, armed robbery, kidnapping, homicide, suicide, theft, and bomb threats.

In 1991, several incidents heightened awareness of violence in hospitals, including the killing of a nurse at Alta View Hospital in Sandy, Utah. A major portion of violent incidents is being tied to the spread of gang activity and to drugs as well as to incidents involving psychotic or disturbed patients or visitors. Hospitals nationwide report that staff, including physicians and nurses, are becoming more and more anxious over the potential for violence.

While most assaults have occurred in emergency departments and psychiatric units, incidents on general patient floors and in community settings also are increasing. In March 1993, for example, a home-care nurse was shot and killed in an affluent suburban home while caring for a respirator-dependent child. As one spokesperson observed to the press, "Nurses in the United States work in a world where violence has infiltrated both the traditional hospital setting and the public health environment."[109]

According to the American Nurses Association, as violence in health care settings escalate, nurses are the health care workers at greatest risk for violence on the job. Among the reasons cited are the following:

- Nursing is a career in which a high percentage of employees are women;
- The nature of the work involves close physical contact and proximity;
- The work is in shifts; and

- The worksite (e.g., hospitals, clinics, etc.) is highly accessible and may not be secure.[110]

A cursory review of literature also indicates that staff cuts put nurses and other health care workers in potentially dangerous situations, especially when they are required to work alone with violent or potentially violent individuals. Staff cuts force workers to deal with too many patients in too little time. As a result, patients deprived of the care and attention they may deserve direct their anger, frustration, and violence at workers who are trying to help them. Moreover, harsh economic times, high unemployment, and general anger at bureaucratic systems further compound the frustrations of the general public. With their patience and tolerance stretched to the breaking point, it is likely that more people are going to lash out verbally and physically.

All nurses need to heighten their awareness of potentially troublesome and/or dangerous situations. A starting point is to ask the following questions:

- Are other people more worried about my workplace safety than I am?

- Am I able to acknowledge the existence of verbal abuse, assaultive behavior, or the potential for violence in my work environment and personal life?

- What are the patterns or trends of violence in my employment setting? Where would I go to obtain this information?

- Am I capable of detecting an increasing level of agitation in a patient or visitor and using verbal de-escalation techniques?

- How would I call for back-up?

- Do I trust my colleagues and other supportive personnel to intervene in a helpful manner?[111]

(A more comprehensive "violence awareness checklist" appears in the June 1993 issue of *The American Nurse*.)

It is also important to press for preventive measures. These measures should include training in reducing aggression and managing assaultive behavior, written policies and procedures on containment of assaultive patients, improved, more effective security, and adequate staffing patterns. Most importantly, however, nurses must be willing to report all assaultive incidents (including grabbing, hitting, choking, kicking, biting, etc.). In turn, employers must encourage such reporting, implement procedures for handling violent episodes, and offer competent treatment to any employee who is injured (physically and/or psychologically) in a violent or assaultive workplace incident.

SUMMARY

Understanding today's work environment is no easy task for nurses and other health care workers. The workplace is undergoing tremendous change as a result of business reorganization, work redesign, and/or implementation of quality controls. Further compounding the situation are the challenges posed by the growing diversity of the workforce and the complexity of workplace issues. Consequently, it is extremely important for nurses to learn to watch for and accurately interpret a broad range of signals.

5

SCRUTINIZE INVOLVEMENT IN WORKPLACE DECISION MAKING

Power is knowing how to work within the system and use the system to reach one's goals.

JANE MEIER HAMILTON AND MARCY E. KIEFER
Survival Skills for the New Nurse[112]

In the past 20 years, tremendous social and technological changes have brought about a "revolution" in management practices. The information explosion, technological innovation, shifting demographics, reordering of priorities, and changes in the work ethic—all contribute to the rising demand for different organizational structures and new leadership styles.

Like other industries, health care organizations have been forced to carefully assess management practices. The push for health care reform, the advent of total quality management and continuous quality improvement (TQM/CQI), patient-centered care initiatives, and the redesign of work processes have necessitated rethinking the relationship of people and systems.

As greater emphasis is placed on effective, cost-efficient organizations, it is essential that nurses play key roles in redesigning health care systems. Nurses need to critically assess the effectiveness of the decision-making arrangements in their work settings. Given the tremendous changes occurring within the industry, it is extremely important to have a clear understanding of the latest organizational models and management theories. This chapter is designed to answer basic questions about management practices, leadership styles, and team building and to offer basic guidelines for effective participation in workplace decision making.

MANAGEMENT TRENDS

Organizations in all industries are becoming more complex and more competitive. According to Kenneth Blanchard et al., "if we are to survive we must figure out ways to tap into the creativity and potential of people at all levels."[113] Many experts contend that realignment of the lines of authority and power is at the heart of more efficient, effective use of personnel.

How are management practices changing within health care organizations?

Since the Industrial Revolution, the common approach to management has been a functional-hierarchical structure. This structure is characterized by a pyramid comprising multiple layers of management with varying levels of authority and control. While this approach was once highly successful, management experts now believe a more flexible organizational structure best meets today's operational needs.

Since the 1980s, there has been greater movement toward decentralization. Rather than "boxing" workers into a rigid structure of lines of authority and power, there is growing support for creating "spheres" of responsibility (i.e., a circular organization) to enable teams of workers to engage more freely in decision making and to allow for greater interaction among teams/groups.[114]

The ultimate objective of this newer approach is to "empower" workers. Empowerment is defined as "the act of building, developing, and increasing power through cooperation, sharing, and working together."[115] The process of empowerment, according to Judith Vogt and Kenneth Murrell, "enlarges the power in the situation as opposed to merely redistributing it."[116]

Within many health care settings (especially hospitals), there have been efforts to "streamline" the organizational structure. Layers of management have been eliminated (i.e., middle managers); pyramid arrangements have been flattened, narrowed, or inverted; and/or the concept of "matrix" organization (cross-referencing of departmental and functional categories) has been introduced. While all of these approaches may be intended to represent major change, some observers contend that "they still look, act and feel like a traditional functional-hierachical organization . . . because the basic organizational infrastructure has not changed."[117]

What are the different approaches to participative management?

As referenced in the previous chapter, participative management is a key ingredient in TQM/CQI. Truly successful quality management programs facilitate a high level of participation in decision making. This means that front-line workers are actively involved in and responsible for decisions.

In most workplaces, there are a number of different decision-making styles in operation. They vary from highly participative to highly restrictive. These styles are best classified in the following manner:

Top-Down—Top-level personnel make decisions and tell individuals at lower levels what the decision is.

Consultative—Top-level personnel make a tentative decision, announce it to the organization and request input.

Consultative-Upward Communication—Lower-level personnel are expected to propose ideas and potential decisions to higher levels; however, the ultimate decision making remains at the higher levels.

Consensus—Decisions are widely discussed and only considered final when everyone agrees that it is the right decision.

Delegation with Veto—Lower-level personnel make decisions as a matter of course; however, top-level personnel retain the power to reject the decision and ask the lower-level personnel to look at it again.

Delegation with Guidelines—Choices are given to lower-level personnel who make decisions within certain constraints. Guidelines for decisions are often given that involve strategy, philosophy, or values.

Pure Delegation—Lower-level personnel are free to make decisions in whatever way they wish.[118]

According to Edward Lawler and others, a useful way to view the potential effectiveness of a participative program is to determine which type of decision-making style is being used, the extent to which information is shared (both upward and downward), and how much of the organization is involved.[119]

For many years, nursing departments have experimented with various approaches to increasing staff nurses' involvement in patient care decision making. Shared governance has been one of the more controversial approaches. According to some observers, a "second generation" of shared governance is emerging.

In an article entitled "Sustaining Work Redesign Innovations Through Shared Goverance," Terry Minnen et al. indicate that there is some movement away from a centralized committee structure (functional-hierarchical structure) toward unit-based boards (circular organization concept) and greater emphasis on multilevel, multidisciplinary collaboration.[120] While more traditional shared governance models have been designed to address professional nursing practice issues, "second generation" models focus more broadly on patient-centered care, continuous improvement, professional practice issues, and quality of worklife issues.[121]

In considering shared governance, a word of caution is in order. Writing in *Current Issues in Nursing*, Meridean Maas and Janet Specht point out that shared governance in nursing has met with mixed success because of "much variation in the organizational models implemented under the label of shared governance."[122] According to Maas and Specht, terms such as *participative management, self-governance, empowerment,* and *professional practice*, at times, are used as synonyms for shared governance. At other times, these same terms are used to denote distinctly different organizational models with varying degrees of nurse participation in workplace decision making.[123]

It is clear that employers have "mixed motives" for implementing shared governance and other forms of participative management. While some employers actually strengthen nursing's authority, many make an effort to increase nurses' participation in decision making without implementing structural changes to give them greater authority and accountability for decisions affecting nursing practice. Moreover, there is growing evidence that employers, wishing to avoid unionization, attempt to enlist staff nurses to serve on committees with personnel functions or other corporate responsibilities or assign them quasimanagerial duties as a ploy to render them ineligible for a bargaining unit.

Maas and Specht emphasize that nurses must become more astute about the distinctions among governance concepts, "so that they are not misled into believing they are sharing governance with management as professionals, when in fact they are not equal partners in meeting the mandates of the profession and the goals of the organization."[124]

It is extremely important for nurses to clearly understand the organizational structure in their workplace. It is equally important to assess the degree of input and involvement nurses actually have in the organization, no matter what approach is being taken. The following questions may assist you in assessing your organizational structure.

Assessing Organizational Structure

- Is the organizational structure characterized by centralized or decentralized control?

- Is there a clear understanding of lines of authority and responsibility? Is this information available in written form?

- What is the nurse executive's role?

- What are the expectations of nurses functioning in leadership roles?

- How many employees report to one supervisor/team leader?

- What degree of power is assigned to work units/teams and workplace committees? Are the decisions of these groups binding or do they merely have the power to recommend?

- What methods of communication are used to convey important information to staff?

- To what extent are nurses represented on workplace committees?

- What methods are used to address/resolve workplace problems and conflicts?

- Is employee morale high, or is there a need for improvement?

- What levels of trust/support do employees display toward the actions of decision-making bodies?

LEADERSHIP STYLES

Involving more and different people in workplace decision making necessitates a new approach to leadership. Such management "gurus" as Kenneth Blanchard, Paul Hershey, Peter Senge, Warren Bennis, Burt Nanus, Tom Peters, Stephen Covey, and others agree that effective leadership involves creating a vision, developing a mission statement, stimulating change, and maximizing individual skills and talents. While the focus was once on controlling and directing, now leadership is about empowering and coaching. This new approach has been given a variety of labels, including "transformational leadership."

Styles of leadership are receiving growing attention in nursing literature. There are a number of variables that have an impact on the role of leaders within the health care arena. As Tim Porter-O'Grady points out, these variables include "new frameworks for thinking about and designing work, changed ways of doing work, and different players involved in undertaking caregiver roles."[125] According to Porter-O'Grady, "the more dynamic, interactive, and synergistic requirements of the emerging age call for a new set of skills and insights on the part of the leader."[126]

What skills must today's leaders possess?

Paul Hershey and Kenneth Blanchard contend that "leadership occurs any time one attempts to influence the behavior of an individual or group regardless of the reason."[127] Management is viewed as "a special kind of leadership in which the achievement of organizational goals is paramount."[128] Within this context, Hershey and Blanchard suggest that there are three general skills or competencies of leadership. First, leaders must be able to understand (*diagnose*) the situation they are trying to influence. Secondly, they must be able to *adapt* their own behavior and other available resources to address whatever circumstances arise. And finally, they must be able to *communicate* effectively.

In *Management of Organizational Behavior, Utilizing Human Resources*, Hershey and Blanchard emphasize that there is no one leadership style that is effective in all situations. The nature of the situation determines the type of leadership behavior that is needed.[129] An understanding of the *situational leadership model* is key to current and emerging approaches to workplace leadership. In situational leadership, three key factors are considered: (1) the amount of guidance and direction a leader gives; (2) the amount of support a leader provides; and (3) the readiness level of followers to perform a specific task or function.[130]

According to Hershey and Blanchard, there are four leadership styles: telling, selling, participating, and delegating. Each style reflects a different degree of task and level of relationship. Using the *telling* style, a leader makes the decisions, provides specific instructions, and closely supervises performance. In the *selling* style, a leader makes the decisions, but greater effort is made to explain decisions and to provide opportunity for clarification. Ideas are shared in the *participating* style. A leader collaborates with followers in making decisions or encourages followers to make decisions. The *delegating* style involves turning over responsibility for decision making and implementation of a plan of action to the followers.[131]

To be most effective in a leadership role, an individual must:

- Decide what individual or group activities are to be influenced,

- Determine the ability and motivation (readiness level) of the individual or group, and

- Identify which of the four leadership styles would be most appropriate.[132]

Within a given structure, how does an individual acquire power?

There are at least five different forms of organizational power. Organizational power is defined as the ability to influence and/or control other employees, decision-making processes, conditions of employment, and other workplace factors.[133]

Organizational Power

Legitimate Power—given to an individual by the organization because of the individual's position in the hierarchy. Usually sanctioned by titles.

Reward Power—based on the ability of an individual to control and administer rewards for compliance with management directives.

Coercive Power—founded on the individual's ability to implement punishments for noncompliance with management's requests.

Expert Power—derived from special abilities, skills, or knowledge demonstrated by the individual.

Referent Power—may stem from two possible sources: the attractiveness or appeal of a certain individual or an individual's connection to or relationship with other powerful individuals.

The amount of influence and control a nurse has depends on the type and source of power established in a particular work setting or situation. Legitimate, reward, and coercive power are given to employees by the employer. Expert and referent power, however, are based on individual characteristics and may or may not be given by the employer.

Nurses also may draw from other sources to build a power base. Nurses may acquire power as a result of their numbers, for instance. As the largest group of health professionals, nurses have the collective power to make a significant impact on a specific work setting or on the health care system as a whole. The holistic approach to care embraced by nurses is a further source of power. Consumers place great value on being treated as whole persons in health care settings. As one health care observer writes, "As nurses continue to demonstrate the kind of care demanded by the public, the power nursing has grows."[134]

The key role nurses play in cost containment also enhances nursing's power. Cost containment is a top priority within the health care industry. More and more, consumers and providers alike are acknowledging the significant impact of nurses as support figures for patients and their families, home health managers, health educators, and monitors of health maintenance. These and other nursing roles are recognized as cost-effective approaches to meeting health care needs. Nurses can use this recognition to strengthen involvement in decision-making processes affecting the delivery of care.

TEAMWORK

Becoming an effective team player (both as a leader and follower) is an important dimension of today's workplace survival skills. No matter what the work setting or role, it is likely that nurses will find themselves more closely involved in some form of group decision making—as part of primary nursing or interdisciplinary care teams, work units, special task forces, and/or committees.

What factors influence team-building in the workplace?

Central to team-building is an understanding of the concepts of work group culture and work group climate. Management theorists define culture as the shared beliefs, values, and assumptions existing in a group. Within an organization, there are apt to be several subcategories of cultures, including corporate culture, managerial culture, professional culture, and work group culture. Work group culture manifests itself in the ways people communicate and interact, the approaches taken to setting priorities, the methods used to deal with power issues, and the extent to which group members work together or alone. According to Harriet Coeling and Lillian Simms, it is "the pattern of behaviors developed by groups to solve work-related problems and survive in their job."[135]

A work group culture is strongly influenced by workers' individual values, personalities, and customary behaviors as well as "critical incidents that have occurred within the history of the group" (e.g., major disagreements).[136] It also may be influenced by the physical arrangement of the work area.

While work group culture is about shared values and expected behaviors, work group climate is a reflection of individual perceptions and feelings about an organization. It is the "personality" of a setting or environment.[137] According to Dominick Flarey in "The Social Climate Scale, A Tool for Organizational Change and Development," work group climate comprises the following specific components of the work environment: involvement, peer cohesion, supervisor support, autonomy, task orientations, work pressure, clarity, control, innovation, and physical comfort.[138] Studies indicate that a positive culture and climate contribute to productivity, job satisfaction, retention, and high morale among workers.

Coeling and Simms point out that "observing and listening provide the richest information about a culture."[139] To learn more about group interaction, Kenneth Blanchard, Donald Carew, and Eunice Parisi-Carew suggest paying close attention to a number of factors, including: patterns of communication and participation; methods of decision making, problem solving, and conflict resolution; style of leadership; and group goals and roles.[140] The following questions may help to assess both the culture and climate in your particular work setting.

- Is it readily apparent that the group shares common beliefs, values, attitudes, and goals?

- Has the group set standards for itself to use in decision making, problem solving, and conflict resolution?

- Are members of the group encouraged and supported?

- Do members' contributions appear to be valued and accepted?

- Are group members brought into discussions and given a chance to be heard?

- Are feelings expressed and are personal issues dealt with?

- Do individual members accept the decisions of the group?

A knowledge of the basic principles of group development is also essential in team-building in the workplace. Considerable research has been done in the area of group dynamics. A wide range of models have been developed to explain the stages of group development. While the number of stages vary among different sources, several common themes emerge.

The first stage of group development involves *orientation*. Each member of the group searches for his or her place within the group. Irwin Yalom refers to this phase as the "in-or-out" time.[141] (Am I going to be a member of this group or am I not going to be a member of this group?) According to Kenneth Blanchard and others, it is a period of testing the situation and key players and of determining individual and group expectations.[142] It is also a time of dependency and reliance on authority and structure.

The next stage deals with *power and control*. According to Yalom, this phase of group development is characterized by conflict, dominance, and rebellion.[143] Group members begin to feel frustration as they experience discrepancies between their initial expectations for the group and the "realities" of the situation. Members may react negatively toward leaders and other group members. There is increasing competition for power and/or attention. Experts agree that it is essential that groups go through this phase. According to Blanchard et al. in *The One Minute Manager Builds High Performing Teams*: "Although this stage is characterized by power struggles and conflict, it also is the seedbed of creativity and valuing differences."[144] However, research does indicate that, if the "infighting" characteristic of this stage is not handled satisfactorily, power and control issues will remain dominant throughout the life of the group.

The latter stage(s) of group development represents a movement toward *cohesion*. As problems and conflicts are dealt with more effectively by the group, the level of trust and support increases. Typically, the quality of listening improves, and people begin to respect each other's contribution. There also tends to be more sharing of responsibility and control.

Every group goes through these stages of development. Various factors also can trigger a regression in a group's development. Changes in group composition, new or very different assignments, and events that disrupt group functioning can cause a cohesive group to slip back into a period of infighting and dissatisfaction.

What are the characteristics of high performance teams?

As greater effort is directed toward reforming the health care system, issues of productivity, cost efficiency, and quality controls continue to receive increasing attention. Concepts and strategies once reserved for business are becoming common topics in health care literature. The concept of high-performance teams is one example. According to Carl Larson and Frank LaFasto in *Teamwork—What Must Go Right/What Can Go Wrong*, high-performance teams are characterized by: (1) a clear and elevating goal, (2) a results-driven structure, (3) confident team members, (4) unified commitment, (5) a collaborative climate, (6) standards of excellence, (7) external support and recognition, and (8) principled leadership.[145]

Team-building entails (1) establishing goals, (2) determining roles and responsibilities, (3) identifying and continually evaluating decision-making processes, and (4) handling intergroup or interpersonal conflict. An effective team is described as an energetic group of people who display commitment to common goals, who interact well with one another, who enjoy working together, and who achieve results. Blanchard et al.'s *One Minute Manager* uses the acronym PERFROM to describe the "essentials" of an effective team. These key elements are purpose, empowerment, relationships and communication, flexibility, optimal performance, recognition and appreciation, and morale.[146]

The following characteristics of productive teams provide a basic framework by which to evaluate your group or team's effectiveness:

- Goals are understood and accepted.
- Individual roles and responsibilities are clearly defined.
- The leadership does not dominate.
- Communication is open and honest and there is a free flow of information.
- The general atmosphere is comfortable.
- Members share responsibility for team leadership and development.
- Members willingly accept assignments and adapt to changing demands.
- There is a distinct process for problem solving and conflict resolution.
- Decisions are reached by consensus.
- Individual and group contributions are valued and recognized.
- There is a strong sense of cohesion and team spirit.[147]

How do you facilitate productive meetings as a group leader?

According to Bill Schul's *How To Be an Effective Leader*, "you will be hailed as a valuable leader if you will see to it that your group follows the recognized steps in clear thinking and assist them in avoiding the dangers of fractured thinking."[148] The key to facilitating productive meetings is to help group members to carefully think through a problem and arrive at the best solution. Philosopher John Dewey identified five steps in this process (often referred to as "reflective thinking").[149]

- Recognition of the specific dynamics which constitute the problem at hand.
- Thorough examination of the problem to determine its nature, scope, and implications.
- Search for a new orientation to the problem.
- Comparison and evaluation of the solutions which seem possible.
- Selection of that solution or course of action which, based upon the foregoing reflection, seems best.

A group leader facilitates this process by suggesting ways of tackling a task, soliciting input (facts, ideas, opinions, and feelings), providing clarification and elaboration, pulling together related ideas, attempting to reconcile disagreements, and drawing all group members into the discussion. The following basic steps are essential to conducting a successful meeting.

Prepare for the Meeting

- Develop an agenda that clearly indicates the purpose and content of the meeting.
- Review the status of all agenda topics.
- Gather all necessary background information and supportive data.
- Determine if any spokespersons should be invited.
- Prepare a list of questions to stimulate interaction on agenda topics.

Shape the Meeting at the Outset

- State the goals and objectives of the meeting in clear, concise terms.
- Provide necessary background information.
- Explain what is expected of the group.
- Set time limits.

Adhere to the Agenda

- Keep the meeting on course by deferring irrelevant topics and postponing discussion of related new topics until later.
- Note key ideas and decisions (internal summaries).
- Honor time constraints.
- Credit group participants who help keep the group focused on the topic under consideration.
- Respond to problem situations immediately (i.e., competing conversations, rambling or dominating participants, etc.).

Conclude the Meeting

- Summarize the discussion.
- Identify any action to be taken and who will be responsible.
- Determine what kind of follow-up is required.

The responsibility of a group leader is not only to push through an agenda, but also to pay attention to the functioning of the group. For example, the physical setting of a meeting has a significant effect on the group's psychological environment, and thus on the outcome of the meeting. When selecting the meeting site, consideration should be given to the size of the room, acoustics, lighting, access to the room, ventilation, and room layout.

How do you facilitate productive meetings as a group participant?

According to Susan Roe, there are two sets of functions that operate in a group at all times.[150] One set of functions focuses on the tasks of the group. In fulfilling these functions, group participants are expected to:

- Review all relevant material before meetings,
- Take an active part in all discussions,
- Share pertinent information and experiences with the group,
- Understand and respect others ideas and conflicting viewpoints,
- Approach problems objectively and impersonally,
- Seek clarification and elaboration as necessary, and
- Accept and follow through on assignments, adhering to deadlines and delegated tasks.[151]

A second set of functions deals with the interpersonal relationships of group members (group dynamics). No matter what charge is given to a group, individual members are likely to assume certain roles. These roles fall into three major categories: group-building roles, group maintenance roles, and group-blocking roles. Among the group-building roles are the initiator, opinion giver, clarifier, and tester:

- The *initiator* suggests new or different ideas for discussion or proposes new or different approaches to problems.

- The *opinion giver* shares relevant beliefs about what the group is considering.

- The *clarifier* gives relevant examples, offers rationales, and searches for meaning and understanding of matters under consideration.

- The *tester* raises pertinent questions to determine whether the group is ready to come to a decision.

Individuals assuming group maintenance roles fulfill distinctly different functions. For example, the *gate keeper* keeps the lines of communication open by encouraging group members to participate. The *tension reliever* interjects humor at appropriate times to draw off negative feelings. The *compromiser* is willing to yield when necessary to ensure the progress of the group.

Unfortunately, while some individuals facilitate the group process, others may actually hinder or block the work of the group by asserting authority (*dominator*), boasting or talking excessively (*recognition seeker*), changing the subject constantly (*topic jumper*), or using group time to draw attention to personal concerns (*special interest pleader*). The greatest shortcoming of these individual participants is poor listening skills. They fail to make worthwhile contributions to group discussions because they do not engage in active listening. Their focus is on some agenda other than the business at hand.

Good listening skills are a key to effective group participation. Active listening, as defined by Barbara Norton and Anna Miller, is "receiving and understanding the obvious and hidden meanings of messages from another person."[152] It involves careful observation of the person who is speaking, and verbal and nonverbal response to the message.

Many individuals do not know how to listen. As one source points out, "we are often guilty of listening for facts or listening intelligently for the verbal statement alone when the art of listening is the discerning of ideas."[153] (Listening skills are discussed at greater length in Chapter 7.)

SUMMARY

Scrutinizing involvement in workplace decision making has never been more important. Management theory and leadership styles are changing to accommodate a more dynamic, competitive work environment. For nurses, these changes can lead to increasing involvement in group decision making and problem solving. To make the most of these opportunities, however, nurses must possess a working knowledge about organizational structures, group dynamics, team-building, and problem-solving processes.

6

RECOGNIZE STRESS AND ITS MANIFESTATIONS IN THE WORKPLACE

Learning to cope with job stress is a process. It is a way of traveling through life, not a destination.

EMILY E. M. SMYTHE
Surviving Nursing[154]

According to Dennis Jaffe and Cynthia Scott, the majority of life stresses fall into four categories. These categories are best described by the words *loss, threat, frustration,* and *uncertainty*.[155] Unfortunately, these are the very words many health care workers use to describe their reactions to the massive changes occurring in the health care industry.

Although nurses are trained to observe stress symptoms in their clients/patients, they may not always apply the same insight to themselves or their colleagues. This chapter serves as a reminder that nurses are also vulnerable to stress. It touches upon important considerations about professional and personal well-being.

STRESS AWARENESS

In the most basic sense, stress is defined as physical or emotional *tension* triggered by a stimulus that requires some type of adjustment. The degree of stress or tension depends on the intensity of the demand to change or adapt.

According to Ronald G. Nathan et al. in *The Doctors' Guide to Instant Stress Relief,* sources of stress (stressors) can be divided into three basic categories: situation, mind, and body.[156] In other words, stressors may be external or internal. External stressors are demands imposed by people, things, and events. Internal stressors are self-imposed: what you think and what you do to and for your body can trigger stress.[157]

What is the common response to stress?

Stressors affect every one differently. What causes anxiety and frustration for one person motivates and energizes another. Physician and researcher Hans Selye defined stress as a "nonspecific response of the body to any demand made upon it."[158] Whether stress has a positive or negative impact is an issue of control. Distress (negative stress) occurs when stress controls you. Eustress (positive stress) occurs when you control stress.

It is important to remember that every source of stress, no matter where it comes from or how it is interpreted is physiologically perceived as a potential threat to safety. According to Selye, the presence of stress triggers a three-phase physiological response ("stress syndrome"):[159]

> ***Excitement or Alarm***—An individual gears up to fight or flee from the stressor ("fight or flight" response).

> ***Resistance***—An individual's body mobilizes its resources to combat stress; the body gives off warning signals (stress symptoms).

> ***Exhaustion***—The individual gives up (stress-related illness; burnout).

Because of the body's automatic reaction to stressors, stress is viewed as a self-protective process.

What are the major job stressors for nurses?

Extensive research has been conducted on the caring professions and workplace stressors. Common stressors among caregivers are long hours, poor pay or promotion prospects, lack of autonomy or involvement in decision making, work overload (either too much or the wrong sort), nonsupportive relationships with colleagues, and ineffective or time-wasting arrangements for dealing with patients.[160] Nurses in a variety of roles and settings acknowledge these and many more concerns.

Over the last few years, new and more pressing demands have been placed on nurses. Under the guise of reform, health care employers continue to look for more ways to maximize staff utilization. In this environment, nurses must continually meet the challenge of demonstrating the economic value of nursing services without compromising the nature, scope, or standards of nursing care.

The delivery of health care services is becoming a more complicated enterprise. Medical advancements and technological innovations pose a continuing need for nurses to broaden their knowledge base and refine their skills. In addition, the growing complexity of health care needs, coupled with the discovery of more types of lifesaving measures, poses a variety of ethical dilemmas.

A source of much of nurses' stress is intrinsic—related to the nature of the work.[161] Intrinsic stressors include dealing with dying patients and death; the threat of infection and disease; exposure to various medicinal and antiseptic substances; shift work; working with new, sophisticated technology; and physical factors such as unpleasant odors, warm temperatures, insufficient ventilation, and excessively high noise levels.[162]

The fact that approximately 97% of nurses are women adds yet another dimension of on-the-job stress. While both men and women are affected by stress in the workplace, women may be disproportionately affected for three reasons:

1. Women tend to have lower-paying jobs and less work-related autonomy than men.

2. More women than men are likely to be affected by competing work and family responsibilities. Women, according to some experts, experience the "dual-day syndrome"—working full-time at a paying job, then working equally hard at home.

3. Women bear a disproportionate amount of stress related to sexual harassment and/or discrimination in wages, training, and promotions.[163]

For these and other reasons, nursing is viewed as a highly stressful occupation.

How does stress manifest itself in the workplace?

Symptoms of stress are generally grouped into five categories reflecting the physical, emotional, intellectual, social, and spiritual dimensions of an individual. Research confirms that everyone manifests symptoms of stress in each of these categories. Given each person's uniqueness, however, the combination of symptoms experienced in a specific situation may vary greatly among individuals. Symptoms within the five categories range from diarrhea to constipation, hostility to apathy, preoccupation to boredom, withdrawal from contact with others to domination of others, and doubt of self-worth to lack of commitment to values.

Research clearly shows a relationship between job stressors and physical, cognitive, and emotional changes in individuals. The most compelling studies demonstrate that psychological stressors produce altered measurements of various bodily chemicals, hormones, and organic functions, as well as altered levels of anxiety.[164] Among other things, these changes can result in a suppressed immune response, leading to a greater frequency of illness.

In highly stressful work environments, a variety of physical symptoms may be common, including occasional or chronic headaches, fatigue, sleep disorders, and ulcers. Common cognitive signs of stress may include inattention, irritability, poor concentration, and problems making decisions. Common emotional reactions to stress may include anxiety, tearfulness, anger, feelings of abandonment, and the sense of being overwhelmed all the time.

Studies indicate that symptoms of stress in the workplace may lead to one or more of the following: absenteeism, tardiness, high turnover, resistance to change, decreased motivation, low morale, disorganization, decreased efficiency, increase in errors, lack of trust among co-workers, passive-aggressive behavior, emotional outbursts, and inability to leave work at work.[165] All of these factors have obvious implications for job performance, productivity, and organizational effectiveness—concepts receiving increasing attention within the health care industry.

Why is burnout a serious issue for nurses?

According to Ayala Pines and Elliot Aronson in *Career Burnout—Causes and Cures*, individuals involved in human services generally share three basic characteristics: (1) they perform emotionally taxing work; (2) they possess certain personality characteristics; and (3) they share a "client-centered" orientation. These three characteristics, according to Pines and Aronson, are "the classic antecedents of burnout."[166] Burnout is the most extreme reaction to workplace stress.

Studies show that individuals entering the nursing field tend to have similar personality traits. According to Diana Gallagher, they are action-oriented, attentive to detail, set high standards for themselves, have difficulty accepting work that is less than perfect, and "are giving to the point that their own health and relationships tend to rank second to patient care."[167] She concludes, "The qualities that provide an unusually high level of dedication and good quality patient care are also the source of potential burnout."[168]

In one study of staff nurses' reactions to stress, researchers discovered that the symptoms most frequently reported included:

- feeling "used up" at the end of the work day,
- feeling emotionally drained from work,
- feeling frustrated by work,
- feeling that worthwhile work as a nurse had been accomplished only a few times a month,
- feeling fatigued when having to get up and go to work,
- feeling burned out,
- feeling that they worked too hard in their roles as nurses, and
- feeling personally involved with patients' problems.[169]

The frequency with which nurses experienced these and similar symptoms ranged from a few times a month to at least once a week. More recent studies document similar findings.

Career burnout is characterized as moving from enthusiastic expectations to disillusionment to anger and frustration and finally to apathy. Behavioral researchers contend that such burnout develops in stages "often so slow and insidious that a nurse may ignore or even deny the problem."[170] How do you guard against this happening to you? Stress awareness, according to Albrecht, (1) leads to better understanding of some experiences as warning signals that require response, (2) improves one's understanding of others' behavior, and (3) triggers the development of stress management strategies.[171]

STRESS MANAGEMENT

Since an estimated 80% of illness is believed to be stress-related, your well-being literally depends on learning to cope with job stress.[172]

What is stress management?

At the heart of stress management is the development of a self-care philosophy that addresses physical, emotional, intellectual, social, and spiritual needs. According to Smythe, this approach fosters self-awareness, personal responsibility, positive self-regard, and a healthy lifestyle.[173] The ultimate objective of stress management is to embrace a holistic approach to living.

Physical fitness, for example, is an important component of a healthy lifestyle. Establishment of a nutritional diet program, adequate rest, and a regular exercise routine are the more obvious strategies for maintaining a healthy body and preventing illness (*physical self-care*).

Experts in psychosomatic medicine report that the most common cause of fatigue and actual sickness is the repression of emotion. Part of *emotional self-care* is learning to experience and express feelings and emotions.

One objective of *intellectual self-care* is to challenge and broaden one's mind. The development of a career plan, for example, is a key motivational factor in the pursuit of additional education and special training.

Developing and maintaining support systems are essential elements in *social self-care.* A networking system places an individual in touch with a group of colleagues who lend support, information, and guidance. Other arrangements, such as mentoring, also foster intellectual stimulation and inspirational support.

Finally, in developing self-care plans, individuals often overlook spiritual needs. The goal of *spiritual self-care* is to facilitate a feeling of inner peace and connection with a "higher power." Selye emphasized the need for "contemplation of something infinitely greater" to defuse daily frustration.[174] It is on the spiritual level that individuals learn to live with stressors over which they have no control.

What are some basic stress coping techniques and strategies?

There are a wide range of approaches to relieving symptoms of stress and handling stressors. It is important to find the approach that is most suited to you. To be most effective, a stress management plan should include measures designed to (1) heighten self-awareness; (2) foster positive thinking; (3) relieve tension; and (4) provide for proper nutrition, exercise, and rest.

Heighten Self-Awareness

It is important to become more in tune with your body's signals of stress. This may be accomplished in a number of ways, including the use of stress and biofeedback cards to obtain instant data on level and/or degree of stress. Nathan et al. suggest routinely checking for the following common indicators of stress: muscle tension, cool hands, nervous sweating, rapid pulse, and shallow and rapid breathing.[175]

According to Jaffe and Scott, another way to increase self awareness is to ask yourself a series of questions about your immediate circumstances:[176]

- How much stress am I experiencing right now?

- How is it affecting the way I am acting?

- What can I do right now to respond to the situation?

- Can anything be done to change the situation or to change my reaction?

- Is it possible to redefine the situation so that it takes on different meaning for me?

These exercises help to pinpoint the basic source of stress (i.e., body, mind, or situation). By knowing where your stress originates, you are better equipped to choose the best tools for relieving it.

These exercises are also helpful in determining your optimal stress level. In proper amounts, stress can be the catalyst for personal and professional growth and development. Workplace studies, for example, indicate that high and low stress contribute to low job performance (overload and boredom, respectively). Moderate levels of stress, on the other hand, contribute to high job performance.[177]

By routinely monitoring your levels of stress, a "healthy midrange" of stress will become apparent. Equipped with this information, you are in the best position to set realistic goals for yourself.

Take Control of Self-Talk

Self-talk is the intrapersonal dimension of communication. Through self-talk, you assign meaning, make assumptions, evaluate experiences, and draw conclusions.

It is your self-talk (internal response) about an event that results in stress, not the event itself. Selye described stress as "a neutral physiological phenomenon."[178] It is the meaning assigned to the external event that determines whether the physiological reaction is motivational or draining.[179]

Jaffe and Scott point out: "Stress is a product of our interaction with our world; therefore we can change the amount of stress we are under by changing our way of seeing things and our response to things."[180] Part of taking control of self-talk is learning to put things into a manageable perspective.

Experts agree that it is important for individuals to admit that they are not totally self-sufficient and that some elements of life are beyond their control. This posture is best reflected in the "Serenity Prayer" popularized by Alcoholics Anonymous: "God grant me the serenity to accept the things I cannot change, courage to change the things I can, and wisdom to know the difference."[181] A similar sentiment is reflected in the "professional renewal concept" for nurses, developed by Buckley and Walker: "Change the things you can and let go of the things you can't."[182]

If you catch yourself listening to "negative thoughts, daydreaming nightmares or feeling overwhelmed," some sources recommend mentally yelling "Stop!"[183] The same result also can be achieved by using a large, imaginary eraser. These "thought-stopping" techniques are intended to enhance self-talk.

Strategies for fostering healthier thoughts include:

- Show greater caution in the use of such verbs as *must, should, ought, owe, have to,* and *deserve.*

- Avoid assigning exaggerated labels to yourself and others (e.g., stupid, clumsy, careless, weak).

- Routinely substitute the word 'challenge' for the word 'problem.'

- Learn to laugh at yourself and the situation.

- Memorize key quotations to serve as a source of motivation and inspiration.

All of these measures are intended to "take the stress out of what you tell yourself and replace it with more productive and pleasurable self-talk."[184]

Practice Stress Reducing Strategies

Reducing stress entails training your body to relax. The most effective approach combines progressive relaxation techniques with breathing exercises and meditation.

Experts agree that what is commonly referred to as stress is more properly labeled tension. It is extremely important, therefore, to become more sensitive to the differences between muscle tension and relaxation. Progressive muscle relaxation techniques involve individually contracting and relaxing each muscle group of the body. There are a number of relaxation tapes available to facilitate this type of conditioning.

When you become aware of a warning signal of stress (e.g. muscle tension, rapid pulse, nervous sweating, etc.), one of the best ways to relax is to "breathe stress away."[185] Simply breathe in slowly through your nose or mouth to the count of five and release the air in the same fashion. Repeat this pattern several times. Most stress management books describe a variety of breathing exercises.

Studies also indicate that meditation can be highly effective in releasing tension. Meditation refers to methods of mental training that focus attention and induce calm. Common types of meditation include mindfulness meditation (focusing on moment-to-moment experiences, noting thoughts, feelings, and sensations) and visualization or object concentration.

While relaxation techniques are very important in reducing stress, it is not necessary to have a daily relaxation routine. According to one source, once a week is probably enough to establish a conditioned response.[186] It is, however, important to identify a few "instant" stress relievers that can be used any time or place as needed. Experts recommend a combination of the following simple activities:

- Take six deep breaths.
- Visualize a favorite place.
- Stretch several times.
- Change the scene by walking to a window or a different part of the room or building or by going outside briefly.
- Take an exercise break (e.g., short brisk walk, climb stairs).

It also has been suggested that a friend may be a good outlet for reducing your stress. However, a word of caution is in order. Do not overwhelm your listener by "unloading" all your issues and concerns. Robert Bolton, in his book on people skills, explores the importance of "dumping one's bucket of tension without filling the other's bucket."[187] Bolton warns against releasing tension in such a manner as to increase the level of tension in the listener(s).[188] This is a particularly important factor in fostering healthy relationships in the workplace.

Eat Right, Get Sufficient Rest, and Exercise Routinely

Proper diet, rest, and regular exercise are also key components of stress management. It is important, for example, to be aware of the fact that a number of chemicals can trigger a stress response. These include caffeine, salt, and sugar. In planning three meals a day, make a concerted effort to:

- Limit cholesterols and saturated fats.
- Avoid foods containing salt and refined sugar.
- Monitor use of caffeine.
- Eat more fiber and fish.
- Take a high quality vitamin/mineral supplement daily.

In addition to adequate amounts of sleep, it is important to schedule breaks during the day. Short rest periods tend to diminish the tension associated with workplace demands. Building in breaks—no matter how short—also provides a sense of control over schedules.

Finally, research shows that physical exercise actually burns off the biochemical by-products of the stress response and contributes to more restful sleep. In developing an exercise regimen, be sure to select a vigorous activity or sport that uses the large muscle groups gradually. No matter what exercises are chosen, trainers recommend stretching before starting each session and ending each session by walking a few minutes to cool down.

A comprehensive plan of stress management also incorporates theories and practices associated with assertiveness training, time management, the grieving process, values clarification, and conflict resolution. These and related topics are discussed separately.

WORKPLACE SUPPORT

According to Jaffe and Scott, job stress results from factors associated with the (1) physical work environment; (2) structure, culture, and values of the organization; and (3) person-to-person environment.[189] Clearly, a personal stress management program alone will not lead to elimination or reduction of all stressors. The effective management of workplace stress requires a combination of individual and organizational measures.

It is equally important for employers to institute policies and procedures and implement programs and services aimed at minimizing stressful conditions. For a workplace stress management program to be most effective, occupational health consultants recommend that employers:

- Identify the various methods individuals use in attempting to reduce or enhance stress;

- Establish a system that allows employees to acknowledge that stress is reaching a limit that will reduce performance; and

- Provide intervention programs that enhance the worker's ability to establish individual methods of coping with stress.[190]

What measures should employers take to reduce workplace stress?

In an article entitled "Manage Nurse Stress and Increase Potential at the Bedside," Patricia Grant notes: "It is counterproductive to allow occupational stress to exist without some systems of checks and balances in progress."[191] After reviewing scientific literature on stress management and the nursing profession, Jacqueline Dionne-Proulx and R. Pepin concluded that "the most helpful actions in terms of stress management for nurses and employees in general are those which combine individual strategies (relaxation, exercise, time management, etc.) and changes in the organizational environment."[192]

As you take stock of your particular work setting, keep the following questions in mind:

- Has an effort been made to match personal characteristics of employees to the culture of the environment (i.e., placement of the right people in the right jobs)?

- Are job descriptions and responsibilities clearly delineated and understood?

- Is there open, honest communication?

- Are training programs offered to orient/prepare individuals for the technical and interpersonal aspects of their jobs?

- Has an effort been made to allow for greater individual autonomy and involvement in decision making?

- Are allowances made for the creation of formal and informal support groups and team-building?

- What type of employee assistance programs are in place?

- Is sufficient attention paid to basic physical factors, such as lighting, ventilation, and furniture and equipment needs?

- Are personal and family needs taken into account?

- Are surveys and other measures periodically initiated to assess levels of stress and pinpoint specific concerns?

These questions are intended to raise your level of consciousness regarding factors contributing to a healthy work environment.

ASSERTIVENESS

Working relationships play an important role in increasing or moderating workplace stress. A number of experts contend that an individual's personal and professional success and happiness depend on the ability to relate to others in a healthy manner.

What can you do to foster healthy working relationships?

A number of books have been written to support the premise that a relationship is only as good as its level of communication. Effective communication, according to Powell and others, occurs only when individuals can honestly tell each other who they are—what they "think, judge, feel, value, love, honor and esteem, hate, fear, desire, hope for, believe in, and are committed to."[193] Studies reveal that most interpersonal conflicts result from repression of feelings and emotions, and most interpersonal encounters are achieved through "some kind of emotional communion."[194]

To ensure effective communication, you must be able to recognize three basic patterns of behavior: passive, aggressive, and assertive. Each pattern has its own unique verbal and nonverbal characteristics. Individuals displaying passive or submissive behavior, for example, tend to ramble or are frequently at a loss for words. Seldom do they say what they mean. Most often they use actions instead of words, hoping someone will guess what they mean. They also have a tendency to shift responsibility to others. Common nonverbal signals include nervous gestures, downcast eyes, and a weak, hesitant voice.

Aggressive behavior falls at the other end of the continuum. It is characterized by "loaded" words, accusations, "you" messages that blame or label, and sarcasm. Individuals displaying aggressive behavior project an air of superiority. There is a demanding tone in their voice. Their expression is cold and their stance is usually stiff and rigid.

Assertive behavior, on the other hand, communicates a sense of strength, openness, and caring. Assertive individuals convey their feelings, say what they want, mean what they say, and accept responsibility for their actions. They tend to be attentive listeners. Their tone of voice is warm and their gestures relaxed.

Psychologists caution that both passive and aggressive behavior may seem to relieve stress instantly, but actually create long-term distress.[195] Passive behavior is equated to "inward flight" and aggressive behavior to "disruptive fight."[196] Assertive behavior, on the other hand, represents a "stay-and-play" approach, which tends to minimize stress over time.

To pinpoint your own pattern of behavior (style of communication), ask yourself the following questions:

Are You Passive?

- Do you tend to be apologetic most of the time?
- Do you have trouble coming to the point?
- Do you have a tendency to shift responsibility to others?
- Are you nervous and fidgety when you are talking to other people?
- Do you say "I mean" and "you know" frequently?
- Is it difficult to maintain eye contact when talking to someone?

Are You Assertive?

- Are you able to express your feelings?
- Do you let others know what you need and want?
- Do you accept responsibility for your actions?
- Are you a good listener?
- Do you maintain eye contact when you are speaking and listening?
- Is your body language consistent with what you are thinking and feeling?

Are You Aggressive?

- Do you have a tendency to blame and label people?
- Do you put others down?
- Do you use "loaded" words?
- Are you ever sarcastic?
- Do you stare past the person you are talking to?
- Does your gesturing often include finger-pointing and clenched fists?

Obviously, honest, open communication in the workplace best manifests itself in assertive behavior. Unlike passive or aggressive behavior, assertion is "that type of interpersonal behavior which enables an individual to act in his own best interest, to stand up for himself without anxiety, and to exercise his rights without denying the rights of others."[197] When acting assertively, individuals seek a balance between their rights and those of others.

Melodie Chenevert, in STAT—*Special Techniques in Assertiveness Training*, readily admits that mastering assertiveness requires a sizable investment in time and effort. Becoming skilled in assertiveness, she notes, "requires study, practice, experimentation, evaluation, more study, and more practice."[198] However, the effort does pay off.

Studies reveal that learning to make assertive responses definitely weakens the anxiety and tension experienced in specific situations. Research also indicates that assertiveness reduces feelings of helplessness and frustration. When individuals engage in assertive behavior, their chances increase for developing such characteristics as inner peace, self-respect, honesty, self-control, independence, and decision-making power and ability.

Gerry Angel and Diane Petronko emphasize that assertiveness is "a way to stop being a victim of situations and systems."[199] In *Developing the New Assertive Nurse*, they point out that through assertive behavior, nurses develop "their own natural resources to give them power and control while developing self-esteem."[200]

Mastering assertive behavior requires a clear understanding and appreciation for a person's basic rights. In *Survival Skills for the New Nurse*, Hamilton and Kiefer warn novice nurses to avoid falling into the trap of thinking that nurses must always put others' needs and rights before their own. "Except in the case of patients," they state, "your rights deserve the same respect and attention as anyone else's. Remembering this helps you handle interpersonal problems assertively."[201]

A variety of sources have identified what they consider to be the basic rights of all people. Commonly referred to as the "bill of assertive rights," the list includes:

- The right to be treated with respect.

- The right to have and express opinion, thoughts, and feelings.

- The right to make decisions and decide what, if any, action will be taken.

- The right to ask for what is needed or desired.

- The right to change one's mind.

- The right to refuse (to say "no" without making excuses or feeling guilty).

- The right to make mistakes.

- The right to say "I don't know" or "I don't understand."

In addition to these, nurses' basic rights include:

- The right to be an equal member of the health care team.

- The right to be informed about what is expected at work.

- The right to a reasonable workload.

- The right to an equitable wage.

- The right to determine one's own priorities.

- The right to give and receive information as a professional.

- The right to question and challenge.

- The right to ask for changes in the system.

- The right to act in the best interest of the patient/client.[202]

Linking a specific right to a particular situation makes it easier to initiate assertive behavior. It is essential that you recognize your rights and take them into account in dealing with challenging situations, problems, and issues as they arise in the workplace.

TIME MANAGEMENT

"There are not enough hours in the day" is a common complaint from individuals experiencing the stress of juggling too many responsibilities and tasks. According to Hamilton and Kiefer, "When you live beyond your limits, you experience the pressure associated with role overload and experience less satisfaction in your daily life."[203]

What role does time management play in stress reduction in the workplace?

Mariann Johnson and Diana Gallagher observe, "If time can be viewed as a tangible resource such as money, time management is the way to invest that resource and collect the biggest possible dividends."[204] From a work perspective, the ultimate goal of time management "is to work smarter, not harder."[205]

How time is used in the workplace is often a matter of resolving conflicts among competing demands. Since certain responsibilities cannot be ignored, it is important to learn how to balance demands by adopting basic time management strategies. According to several sources, a systematic approach to using time helps to develop better time management habits which, in turn, foster a greater sense of accomplishment.[206]

Organizational skills play a key role in managing time effectively. Within the workplace, time management involves:

- Listing the aspects of a job that are liked and disliked to better understand the values assigned to certain duties and functions.

- Sorting out (prioritizing) what will or will not be done in a given period of time.

- Writing a "to do" list of the tasks to be accomplished each day ("must do," "do if time permits," "do if all else is completed," etc.).

- Experimenting with a variety of organizational strategies to determine what works best.

To assist nurses in this process, Hamilton and Kiefer have developed a series of questions to help identify job priorities:[207]

- Will patients be jeopardized if this task is not done?

- Is this task a priority because of time deadlines?

- Is this task a key responsibility of the job—one of the elements upon which evaluation is based?

- Do safety concerns make this task a priority?

- Do any legal or regulatory issues make this task a priority?

- Could this task be done by anyone else?
- Will problems arise if this task is postponed?

Most effective time managers create a "to do" list. One of the values in developing such a list is being able to cross off items as they are completed, thus providing a visible gauge of how much has actually been accomplished. There are, however, certain guidelines that should be followed:

- List only specific, time-limited tasks.
- Structure daily activities with energy levels in mind. Plan to undertake tasks that demand precision or concentration during high-energy times.
- Avoid scheduling time so tightly that every minute is accounted for.
- Reserve at least 30 minutes per workday as unscheduled time to accommodate crises, emergencies, and delays.
- Make time for short breaks and for eating lunch. Avoid spending this time in conversations about patients and work problems.
- Also consider scheduling a 15-30 minute "decompression" period of relaxation time between work and home.

Once a routine of using "to do" lists is established, it is important to periodically evaluate the progress being made in improving time management habits. Merrill Douglass and Phillip Goodwin recommend use of the following questions in analyzing time management:[208]

- What was the least productive period of the day? Why?
- What caused the most interruptions?
- What were the three biggest time wasters in a given day?
- How much time was spent in high-value activity?
- How much time was spent in low-value activity?
- What activities could have been accomplished in less time and still produced acceptable results?
- What activities needed more time?

SUMMARY

Recognizing stress and its manifestations in the workplace is of utmost importance to nurses. Coping with job stress requires heightened self-awareness, coupled with fine tuning of communication skills and organizational abilities. Stress management should be viewed as an ongoing process. The most effective stress management plans combine individual strategies and changes in the work environment.

7

LEARN TO MANAGE WORKPLACE CONFLICTS

Successfully handled, conflict allows for the expression of strongly held ideas or feelings that otherwise might not become known.

ELIZABETH ARNOLD AND KATHLEEN BOGGS
*Interpersonal Relationships: Professional
Communication Skills for Nurses*[209]

The development of a positive work climate hinges on the quality of workplace relationships. According to Roe, "positive relationships with others in the work setting . . . are equally as important as the fine tuning of clinical skills."[210]

The establishment of rapport among workers, the development of collegial relationships, and a sense of teamwork are greatly affected by three key processes: values clarification, conflict resolution, and assertive communication. Taken together, they influence the *cohesiveness* of work groups. This chapter explores all three processes, offering basic tips for fine tuning both intrapersonal and interpersonal skills.

VALUES CLARIFICATION

There are at least four value systems in operation in the workplace: personal/professional, work group, organization, and client/patient. Each time a problem or issue arises, these value systems have an impact on the choices made.

According to Shirley Steele, a value is "a standard or criterion for guiding action, for developing and maintaining attitudes toward relevant objects and situations, for morally judging self and others, and for comparing self with others."[211] While individuals may articulate values in different ways, they are a reflection of one thing— that which is most important, most worthwhile, and most cherished.

Professional values are a reflection and an expansion of personal values. According to many sources, what nurses value and how they integrate those values into their professional lives influence their concept of the profession and the quality of care given.[212]

The key characteristics of "high performance" work teams hinge on values (i.e., elevating goals, unified commitment, collaborative climate, standards of excellence, and principled leadership). According to Peters and Waterman, the mark of excellence in organizations is the extent to which a system of common and shared core values is in place.[213]

How are values formed?

Values may be self-directed or other-directed. Other-directed values are influenced by family and significant others, including teachers, co-workers, peers, and other influential people. Other-directed values are usually incorporated into one's value system as a means of achieving acceptance and approval from significant others. Self-directed values, on the other hand, evolve as a result of the internal processing of experiences, feelings, and beliefs.

While personal values vary greatly from one person to another, basic needs are considered to be shared values. The needs for survival, security, esteem from self and others, love and belonging, and self-actualization are valued by all people regardless of age, sex, ethnic group, or religious background. In fact, behavioral scientists contend that values serve as motivators for basic need satisfaction.[214]

Identifying and owning a value is "valuing." In *Meeting Yourself Halfway: 31 Values Clarification Strategies for Daily Living,* Sidney Simon focuses on three concepts associated with acquiring values: choosing, prizing, and acting. According to Simon, before something can be incorporated fully as a value, it must meet a seven-step criteria. It must be:

- chosen freely,
- chosen from among alternatives,
- chosen after due reflection,
- prized and cherished,
- publicly affirmed,
- acted upon, and
- part of a pattern that is repeated.[215]

A belief, attitude, or feeling becomes a value if all seven steps are satisfied.

Values are developmental in nature and change over time. Research indicates that self-directed values (those values influenced by internal sources) are more subject to change and refinement and are less rigid over time.[216] The way in which values are prioritized also changes over time as a result of experience and/or circumstances.

How do you determine what your values are?

According to Diane Uustal, values clarification is "a theory, a process, and a collection of tools designed to assist each of us to find our own answers to a variety of questions and areas of concern in our lives."[217] Values clarification serves several purposes. It can be used to heighten awareness of values and underlying motivations that guide actions. It helps uncover incongruencies between words and actions. It can be used to identify, examine, and analyze conflicting beliefs and feelings that cause tension and create conflict. By prioritizing values, values clarification also facilitates choice making.

No matter what purpose values clarification serves, the overriding objective is to facilitate self-understanding. The following strategies are intended to help identify and clarify your value system.

Develop a Mission Statement

According to Stephen Covey, "one of the single most effective tools for living a principle-centered life is a mission statement."[218] Covey suggests a number of advantages in writing a mission statement. It forces you to think more deeply about your life. It necessitates that you clarify your values and aspirations. It imprints your values and purposes firmly in your mind. By integrating your mission statement into daily planning, it keeps that vision constantly before you.[219]

Test the Strength of Existing and Emerging Values

Create a rating scale using the seven-step criteria discussed earlier (e.g., chosen freely being worth one point and repeated behavior seven points). As you evaluate to what degree a value meets each of the criteria, keep in mind that a true value is acted upon in a consistent manner.

Practice Inward Reflection

According to Hamilton and Kiefer, because of the strong influence of others, you may be out of touch with your "internal signals."[220] They offer the following advice:

- Go beyond a conscious level and listen to your intuitive reactions.

- Tune out the externally created rules or quotes in your head (e.g., shoulds and oughts) and learn to listen to your internal responses to a situation.

- Pay attention to the replay of your thoughts.

- Trust your beliefs, preferences, likes, and dislikes.

- Heed what you are telling yourself and take responsibility for making choices. In other words, act on your internal responses.

- Think of your options as fluid and flexible.

- Establish behavior consistent with your values.[221]

How do you use this information constructively in the workplace?

Values clarification makes a tremendous difference in the way individuals approach conflict and address issues and problems.

Values clarification = self-awareness = rational decision making

Identification of values is at the heart of self-awareness. It is a key to self-actualization.

Values clarification also enhances understanding and acceptance of others. As one source notes: "When you come to know your own values, the boundaries between your feelings and those of others become clear."[222] As a result, it is possible "to respect the individuality of another person, to accept different or mutual feelings, and to be open to the value framework of the other person."[223]

Values clarification facilitates rational decision making and minimizes struggles over ethical dilemmas. According to Uustal, "the clearer we are about what we value, the better equipped we are to choose thoughtfully from among competing alternatives."[224] Studies confirm that when values go unexamined or values conflicts are ignored, the result is "confusion, indecision, and inconsistency."[225]

Finally, personal inventory and values clarification are considered foundation exercises in goal setting. Most management experts agree that effective goal setting is key to motivation and success. By linking goals to values and continually keeping those goals in view, it is possible to stay focused and maintain a sense of direction.

CONFLICT MANAGEMENT

Conflict is bound to arise in the normal course of any employment. Webster defines conflict as "a mental struggle resulting from incompatible or opposing needs, drives, wishes, or demands."[226] Conflict may represent two or more opposing feelings about a situation, person, or idea within a particular individual or signify differences in approaches, feelings, or ideas between two or more individuals.

When conflict is *intra*personal, values clarification and basic stress management techniques are useful tools. There are several different approaches to addressing *inter*personal conflict, some of which are more effective than others.

Vicki Lachman points out that the ability to resolve conflicts with others is an important stress-reducing skill.[227] Whether conflict is managed, suppressed, ignored, or avoided contributes significantly to effective performance in the workplace.

It is readily acknowledged that conflicts often arise within the therapeutic relationship between nurse and client. In fact, a number of books have been written on effective nurse-client communication. Given the complexity of this type of interaction, it is important for nurses to pay close attention to the quality of client relationships. In keeping with the general focus of this publication, however, the following sections explore strategies for fostering healthy relationships among workplace colleagues—between nurses, nurses and supervisors, nurses and physicians, nurses and other health care personnel, or nurses and administrative staff.

What causes conflict to escalate?

Common synonyms for "conflict" include the following: *differ, disagree, contend, contest, argue, cross swords, lock horns, squabble, quarrel, feud, bicker, have words, struggle,* and *do battle.* Careful examination of these words reveals varying degrees or levels of interaction.

Studies indicate that there are several stages of conflict. At the lowest level, there is openness to data gathering and an interest in problem solving. Next, there is a willingness to negotiate, if a solution is not achieved. If compromise is impossible, the conflict turns into a contest in which someone must win or lose. If neither party is willing to be the loser and impasse occurs, the "fight or flight" response kicks in. Finally, the objective shifts from simply wanting to win to wanting to hurt. By this stage, the conflict has reached the point of mutual destruction.

William Hendricks suggests that workplace conflicts fall into three basic categories. There are *day-to-day irritations* that warrant a "wait-and-see attitude." There are challenges (or problems) that give way to a "win-lose mentality." And situations perceived as battles trigger a "fight response."[228]

No matter what labels or stages are assigned to conflict situations, the following points are clear:

- Open communication and the sharing of information are key factors in conflict management.

- Conflict can be productive if contained at the lowest levels.

- Conflict becomes destructive when the parties involved confuse issues and personalities.

- As conflict escalates, every effort must be made to draw it back to a lower level of intensity.

It is equally clear that the ultimate level of conflict rests with the individual. Depending upon how you deal with the emotional dynamics of conflict, you either escalate or deescalate the situation.[229] Consequently, it is important to pay close attention to the way in which you process your own feelings and reactions during conflict. Consider your responses to the following questions:

- How do you know when there is a conflict—what does it look and feel like to you?

- Is your reaction automatic or do you take time to reflect upon the situation?

- Do you find yourself looking for "hidden" meanings in messages? (e.g. Do you frequently ask: What do you think she meant by that? Why do you think he did that?)

- When conflict escalates, do you have a tendency to: place the blame elsewhere? repress your true feelings? withhold information? direct your anger at people rather than issues?

Greater awareness and understanding of your own reactions to conflict ultimately enable you to understand others and to facilitate constructive interaction.

What are the sources of conflict in the workplace?

According to Jaffe and Scott, workplace conflicts fall into three broad categories: structure, communication, and personal behavior.[230] *Structural conflict* results "from roles and barriers that are built into the organizational system."[231] Factors such as role definitions, geographical and physical relationships, unequal power and authority, and unequal control of resources can produce conflict.

Research indicates that *breakdowns in communication represent* the single greatest problem in organizational systems. Poor communication, lack of information, misinformation, different views on what is relevant, and different interpretations of data can lead to misunderstandings and other difficulties.

Personal behavior is a third potential source of conflict. Individuals may refuse to cooperate or become part of the team. Individuals may experience discomfort and tension as a result of conflicting values and strong emotions. The existence of misperceptions or stereotypes may inhibit interaction.

The ability to identify the nature and source of conflict is one more piece of information that helps to better understand and effectively function in any setting.

What methods of conflict resolution are used in the workplace?

Methods commonly used to resolve conflict in the workplace include dominance and suppression, restriction, smoothing, majority rule, compromise, and integrative problem solving. According to Laura Douglass and others, all of these methods are used at some time by managers, but the integrative approach (also referred to as collaboration) offers the most constructive way to resolve conflict.[232]

Integrative problem solving is particularly effective in resolving interpersonal problems that arise from conflicting needs. According to Robert Bolton, the key to this approach is to arrive at "a clear, concrete, succinct statement of the problem" at the outset of the process.[233]

Integrative problem solving involves six basic steps:[234]

1. Define the problem in terms of needs rather than solutions.

2. Use brainstorming to arrive at possible solutions.

3. Select the solution that best meets both parties' needs and check possible consequences.

4. Plan who will do what, where, and by when.

5. Implement the plan.

6. Evaluate the problem solving process and review, at a later date, how well the solution turned out.

Bolton and others have found that this method is "successful with an extraordinary high percentage of typical problems which occur between people."[235] Other basic approaches to conflict resolution, however, have a number of shortcomings.

An underlying characteristic of *dominance and suppression* is a marked class or status distinction between the individuals or groups involved. Dominance and suppression strategies tend to repress interaction by forcing conflict underground and creating a situation in which one side is forced to give way to a higher authority. Emphasis is placed on the immediate conflict rather than on relationships and the long-term effect of the parties' differences.

Restriction is another coercive style of conflict resolution. The objective is to create a situation in which a person in authority tells others what to do and what not to do. Managerial power and strength are used to dictate the actions of others. In this approach to conflict resolution, organizational values (as defined by the manager), cooperation, and teamwork are emphasized. As Douglass points out, "while these are all important and every organization must have them, when overdone, they become destructive."[236]

A slightly more diplomatic way of suppressing or restricting conflict is to employ *smoothing* behavior. An attempt is made to persuade one side to give in to the other side. This tactic, however, is viewed as a short-term strategy. It is likely to trigger feelings of resentment and hostility because the underlying conflict is never resolved, only passed over temporarily.

Some organizations strive to employ staff who are substantially in agreement on major issues and goals. This tactic reflects an *avoidance* approach to conflict resolution by attempting to create a situation in which no differences exist or are likely to arise. The risk of this "mutual admiration society," according to Douglass, is the danger of falling in a "rut of complacency."[237] In this situation, there is little opportunity for creativity, initiative, or growth on the part of the organization or individual employees.

The avoidance approach is also in operation when individuals are unwilling to take a position regarding a conflicting issue. The prevailing sentiment, usually, is: "If we don't talk about it, the problem will go away." Others may embrace the "ostrich in the sand" approach of pretending that a conflict does not exist. Because conflicts are never resolved, resentment builds to a major crisis. Constant staff turnover may result as one means of indirectly resolving the inevitable personal conflicts that build over time.

Some managers try to resolve conflict by the principle of *majority rule.* Experts agree that the elective process can be used successfully if a group has the right to vote, and all group members are willing to abide by the decision. Unfortunately, if one side consistently outvotes the other, the losing side will feel dominated and suppressed. Moreover, many nursing leaders question the feasibility of this approach in a health care setting, since nurses and other workers have certain obligations to meet, no matter what the majority may decide.

Compromise is yet another method of conflict resolution. Unlike the previously mentioned approaches, both parties make concessions as a means of settling differences. Striking a compromise necessitates that each party give up something to meet halfway. In many cases, individuals have difficulty in fully supporting the decision reached through compromise. They often look for opportunities to raise their point of view at a time when it is most likely to "win the other side over." Many management experts view compromise as a weak conflict resolution method because the process is less apt to reach a firm, purposeful solution that will best help the organization to stay on course and achieve its goals.

Dominance and suppression, restriction, smoothing, avoidance, and majority rule are regarded as win-lose approaches to conflict resolution. Compromise, on the other hand, is viewed as a lose-lose approach. Methods that embrace win-lose and lose-lose strategies of conflict resolution have several characteristics in common. According to Filley, these strategies reflect the following shortcomings:

Why Win-Lose and Lose-Lose Strategies Fail

- There is a clear we-they distinction between the parties, as opposed to a we-vs.-the problem orientation.

- Each party sees the issue only from its own point of view. No effort is made to define the problem in terms of mutual needs.

- Emphasis is placed on reaching a solution, rather than on a definition of goals, values, or motives to be attained with the solution.

- Conflicts are personalized; no attempt is made to look objectively at the facts and issues.

- The parties are conflict-oriented rather than relationship-oriented. They emphasize the immediate disagreements rather than emphasizing the long-term effect of differences and how they are resolved.[238]

Experts agree that the most desirable approach to conflict resolution is integrative problem solving, in which the parties involved recognize that conflict exists and openly try to solve the problem that has arisen between them. This win-win model for conflict resolution is characterized by:

- clear definition of values, purpose, and goals;

- open and honest communication of facts and feelings;

- a sense of responsibility among all who participate; and

- an environment of trust and commitment by all to the success of the process.[239]

Within this collaborative framework, each person's position is clear. As conflicts arise, the emphasis is on a group solution in order to build a positive work environment.

INTEGRATIVE PROBLEM SOLVING

How do you facilitate integrative problem solving?

Reactions to conflict situations usually fall into three categories: (1) some individuals may underreact, responding with indirect and vague comments (passive behavior); (2) others may overreact, lashing out with judgmental and evaluative statements (aggressive behavior); and (3) still others may address the situation in an honest and direct manner through open communication (assertive behavior).

Passive and aggressive behaviors tend to be defensive in nature and do little to resolve workplace conflicts. Assertive behavior, on the other hand, encourages collaborative interaction, making it possible to turn conflicts into problem-solving situations (integrative problem solving).

To encourage assertive behavior, it is important to deal with the emotional dimension of conflict at the outset. Bolton recommends a three-step process which "helps people fight constructively—in a systematic, noninjurious, growth-producing way."[240] The steps are: treat the other person with respect (adult-to-adult interaction); listen until you "experience the other side"; and state your views, needs, and feelings.[241]

David Johnson also suggests the following guidelines when laying the groundwork for integrative problem solving:

- Describe the conflict as a mutual problem to be solved, not a win-lose struggle.

- Describe the conflict as specifically as possible.

- Identify differences between concerned parties before attempting to resolve the conflict.

- Reach an agreement about how the conflict is to end and not recur.[242]

The identification of individual needs plays an important role in integrative problem solving. Before a conflict can be perceived as a mutual problem, there must be recognition and understanding of each person's needs. Lachman offers the following advice in the initial stage of defining conflict as a mutual problem:

Assert your own needs, listen reflectively until you understand the other person's needs, and then state both sets of needs in a one-sentence summary of the problem.[243]

The same information base that is used to classify patient/client health needs can be applied to conflict situations in the workplace. Abraham Maslow's well-known theory of self-needs, for example, offers a framework for categorizing needs as they emerge in conflict situations.[244] According to Maslow, there are five categories of needs and wants which cause individuals to think, act, and respond as they do. Maslow emphasizes that the lower level needs (physiological, safety, and belongingness) must be largely fulfilled before higher level needs (esteem and self-actualization) become operative. Maslow's theory provides insight into the level and potential intensity of certain needs (hierarchy of human needs).

Once the problem is clearly defined, it is also important to encourage brainstorming as a method of arriving at the most comprehensive list of possible solutions. The purpose of brainstorming is to creatively generate ideas. In a brainstorming session, each person works individually and writes as many solutions as possible. These solutions are then listed on a blackboard or chart so that everyone can see them. Individual members of the group then build on these ideas to form new and expanded solutions. The basic ground rules for brainstorming are:

- List every idea; do not censor.

- Do not remark or critique anyone's ideas.

- Do not seek clarification or attempt to clarify ideas; it interferes with the creative process.

- Avoid attaching people's names to the ideas they suggest or listing each person's contribution separately.[245]

Once all the viable options or alternatives have been identified, it is equally important to agree upon criteria by which to evaluate each option. This step helps to ensure ownership of the selected solution and, in turn, a higher level of commitment to taking action.

Finally, time should be set aside to review the problem-solving process and assess the effectiveness of the solution (outcome). This activity is crucial to ongoing team-building.

ASSERTIVE COMMUNICATION

Everything that happens in the workplace is influenced by the quality of communication. Communication is commonly defined as "the exchange of meanings between and among individuals through a shared system of symbols that have the same meaning both for the sender and the receiver of the message."[246] These symbols include both verbal and nonverbal forms of communication.

If you wish to enhance your interpersonal skills in the workplace, you must understand the communication process and apply basic communication theory. As Angel and Petronko point out:

Your interpersonal effectiveness depends on your ability to communicate clearly what you want to communicate, to create the impression you wish to create, and to influence the other person in the manner you intend.[247]

How do you facilitate effective workplace communication?

The failure to convey clear, complete messages is perhaps the biggest barrier to communication. According to Johnson, "being complete and specific seems so obvious, but often people do not communicate the frame of reference they are using, the assumptions they are making, the intentions they have in communicating, or the leaps in thinking they are making."[248]

For communication to be effective in the workplace (as in any other setting), it must be carefully thought out. There are certain basic questions that must be answered when preparing to share information in any form:

Purpose

What is the purpose or objective of sharing this information? What is the one most important point to be made?

Organization

What are the major points to be shared and in what order should they be presented?

Content

Is the information to be shared complete? Does it convey "who, what, where, when, why, and how"?

Word Choice

Has careful consideration been given to the choice of words?

In the planning stage, responses to these questions help to shape the content of the message. Once the message is actually formalized, these questions serve as a means of assessing the potential effectiveness of the communication.

It is also important to recognize that the manner in which information is shared and in which ideas and feelings are revealed has a significant impact on problem solving and conflict resolution. Communication experts contend that conflict need not result in a hostile encounter if individuals are willing to engage in open, honest dialogue—assertive communication. Angel and Petronko emphasize that "assertiveness is not a method to gain control over others or to 'beat the system,' but rather is a way of dealing with others in a self-satisfying and respectful way."[249]

Basic rules for assertive communication include the following *tips for communicating information*:

- Take the receiver's frame of reference and perspective into account in structuring a message.

- Provide all information the receiver needs to comprehend the message.

- Assume ownership of the message by using personal pronouns when expressing thoughts, feelings, reactions, and needs.

- Be descriptive when communicating feelings.

- Describe other people's actions without making value judgments.

- Make sure nonverbal signals are congruent with the verbal message.

- Maintain direct eye contact and erect posture.

- Use gestures and facial expressions for emphasis.[250]

Feedback in assertive communication is equally as important as construction of the message. According to Bolton, "vital relationships involve both asserting and listening."[251] In *People Skills: How to Assert Yourself, Listen to Others, and Resolve Conflicts*, he states: "To the extent that either listening or assertion is missing from either person in their relationship—to that degree the relationship falls short of its potential."[252]

Assertiveness trainers suggest the following *guidelines for responding to information:*

- Consider carefully the motives for giving and receiving feedback.

- Give feedback when it is desired.

- Be descriptive rather than judgmental.

- Be specific rather than general.

- Be honest and direct.

- Use personal pronouns when stating feelings or opinions.[253]

In offering feedback, it is also important to deal with things that can be changed. According to Filley, "feedback is most effectively used when it concerns behavior which the recipient can change."[254]

What is active listening?

A majority of misunderstandings in the workplace can be traced to poor listening. Research shows that, on the average, individuals listen at a 25% level of efficiency.[255] Consequently, it is extremely important to develop effective listening skills.

Improving listening habits begins with an understanding of the distinction between hearing and listening. Hearing is a sensory experience—the gathering of sound waves indiscriminately. Listening, on the other hand, is the interpretation of sound. It takes energy to listen. As S. I. Hayakawa points out: "Listening requires entering actively and imaginatively into the other person's situation and trying to understand a frame of reference different than your own."[256]

A good listener looks at the person speaking, asks questions for clarification, shows concern for feelings, repeats some things that are said, pays close attention, reacts responsively, is emotionally controlled, and does not rush or interrupt the person speaking.

How do you make sure you model these characteristics?

Look upon communication as a learning opportunity. Ask yourself: what can I gain/learn from this individual?

Mentally and physically prepare to listen. Turn off the conversation in your head about what you will say and do next. Stop what you are doing and look toward the person speaking. Be sensitive, however, to the fact that eye contact, distance of separation, and touch may enhance or impede communication depending on personal circumstances and cultural orientation.

Take into account both ideas and underlying feelings. Listening for the facts is only part of the process.

Consider the nonverbal as well as the verbal message. Studies indicate that impressions of individuals are primarily derived from facial expression and voice tone.

Make an effort to see the situation from the other person's point of view. Many communication problems arise because of failure to recognize that individual experiences are never identical.

Concentrate on evaluating the message. A listener has the capacity to process considerably more information in a minute than an individual can communicate. Listeners have a tendency to slip into self-talk. As a result, listening becomes selective. To avoid this trap, practice filling in the blanks in a message and evaluating the logic and credibility of the information.

Offer feedback. It is important to listen responsively—to offer feedback as appropriate through both body language and verbal expression. Seek clarification by asking questions. Say in your own words what you heard the other person saying. Try to include some of what you perceive the other person to be feeling. Give the other person a chance to verify your observations.

By channeling your listening energy, you avoid reacting emotionally to the person, topic, or words; prevent hearing what you want to hear; being biased in your listening; and jumping to conclusions, all of which are common barriers to effective communication in the workplace.

How do you communicate with "difficult" people?

One of the most popular training programs today is "dealing with difficult people." Experts tend to use a variety of labels to categorize the degrees and levels of difficult behaviors. Each label or category reflects a distinct set of traits and characteristics. Upon careful study, however, a common theme emerges. More often than not, a "difficult" person is simply an individual who has decided not to listen. No effort is made to be understood or to be understanding.

Given this insight, there are a number of strategies that may be used to draw such individuals into constructive dialogue. The following are a few guidelines:

- Remember that you only have control over your own behavior.

- Never tell someone to "calm down," instead model calmness.

- Think before you speak—take time to process the verbal and nonverbal signals; decide what you want to accomplish in any exchange.

- Do something deliberate to get the individual's attention. Lower your voice, physically move, get the person to sit down.

- Be patient. Allow sufficient time for "blowing off steam."

- Don't argue or disagree, instead ask questions. Force the individual to choose between a conversation or a debate.

When the basic rules of assertiveness are followed in the workplace, the quality of relationships improves. And when properly used, assertive communication facilitates information sharing, problem solving, and conflict resolution in the workplace.

SUMMARY

Learning to manage workplace conflict fosters good working relationships which, in turn, ensure a positive work environment. Through the effective use of values clarification, conflict resolution, and assertive communication, nurses can develop a sense of control (empowerment) in difficult situations. By encouraging honest, open communication and integrative problem solving in the workplace, nurses serve as role models for others.

8

PREPARE FOR TOMORROW

{The 1990s} will be a decade punctuated with revolutionary changes, continued uncertainty, a climate of urgency, great organizational instability and a continuous assault upon and erosion of traditional approaches.

MARGARET D. SOVIE
"Redesigning Our Future: Whose Responsibility Is It?"[257]

Judging from the trends within the health care industry, change is definitely the rule rather than the exception. As Jo Manion points out: "Health care organizations today face a critical choice: innovate and change or expect to be replaced by organizations that do."[258]

This final chapter explores change management and career development. It looks at strategies for dealing with a dynamic, ever-changing work environment and outlines basic guidelines for insuring professional growth and development.

CHANGE MANAGEMENT

One of the greatest challenges facing nurses today is learning to "thrive" amid unprecedented change. As Porter-O'Grady notes, "the person of today is not simply dealing with a great deal of change; instead, people are managing a complex of multiple changes in their lives, most of which are not of their own making."[259]

What is the most common reaction to change?

Studies show that important planned changes invariably produce discomforts and arouse opposition. According to sociologist Robert Merton: "If everyone is comfortable about a proposed change, you may be reasonably certain that it is either a change merely in appearance and not in actuality, or that it is a change so long overdue that it will occur without plan."[260]

Organizations as well as individuals establish "comfort" zones. These comfort zones are said to encompass those beliefs and behaviors that are most valued.

According to JoEllen Goertz Koerner and Sandra Schmidt Bunkers, when change is introduced into a comfort zone(s), "resistance serves as the protection from ideas and actions that we fear might threaten us or destroy our valued relationships."[261]

Organizations, like individuals, tend to have their own unique reactions to planned and unplanned change. Some organizations assume a reactive posture, viewing change as a threat or loss of control. Other organizations are proactive, responding to change by carefully planning for it.

Certain organizational characteristics signal the degree of receptivity or resistance to change. Style of management is likely to have the greatest impact on an organization's response to change. The nature of the mission statement, flexibility of structural arrangements, effectiveness of communication systems, availability of training opportunities, and morale of staff also are indicators of an organization's readiness to deal with change.

Individuals frequently resist change, particularly in the workplace because they like the security of the status quo. As one source points out: "By its very nature, change connotes some degree of risk and may require persons to try out or learn something new. As a result, change may be perceived as a frightening event."[262] Resistance to change also may result from personal attitudes toward change, fear of the unknown, fear of change itself, or some myth or assumption about the outcome of a particular change.

Over the years, several writers have explored the reactions of nurses and other workers to change. Nurses frequently report the following reasons for resisting changes in the workplace:

- a lack of clarity about what the change is,

- a perceived threat from the change agent,

- a feeling that the process and the result of the change have not been thought through,

- selective perception and retention (hearing and remembering only what one wishes),

- too much work involved,

- fear of failure or disorganization,

- lack of two-way communication, and

- a belief that the change seems to benefit the change agent, not necessarily the group.[263]

It is extremely important to be aware of the variety of factors which may influence your reaction to change.

Is it possible to anticipate change?

In interviewing successful people in a wide range of occupations and roles, Peter Drucker, Warren Bennis, Stephen Covey, Anthony Robbins, and others discovered one common trait. Successful people consistently anticipate change before it occurs and are prepared for it.

How do you go about cultivating an awareness of the health care industry and your workplace which allows you to anticipate changes in the making? KEEP

YOUR EYES AND EARS OPEN! Develop the mindset that you will expose yourself to as much information as possible about the health care industry, nursing profession, and work environment. The following are a few basic guidelines:

- Read a variety of national and local newspapers and magazines on a regular basis.

- Subscribe to magazines that follow trends in society.

- Go to a health sciences library routinely to scan a wide range of nursing and health care journals.

- Take note of the issues receiving the greatest attention from hospital, medical, nursing, and other health-related groups.

- Assume an active role in one or more professional organizations.

- Read the current thinking on leadership, management, and marketing.

- Stay apprised of employment rights and protections. Workplace laws and regulations are continuously evolving.

- Study projections regarding demographics, workforce concentration, and technological and medical advances.

- Know your employer. Familiarize yourself with the mission statement, annual reports, policies and procedures, composition of the board of trustees, etc.

- Keep up with the local job market. Follow what is happening at other facilities in the area through networking.

It is through this broad range of information that trends surface and early signals of change become more apparent. Equipped with this knowledge, you are in a better position to distinguish between long-range solutions and "quick fixes" to workplace issues and concerns.

How do you adapt to change?

It is a natural tendency to hold tight to the status quo. While reform of the health care system poses tremendous challenges, it also holds extraordinary opportunities for those who are ready to move forward. Consequently, it is crucial that nurses learn how to deal constructively with change. As Florence Nightingale once wrote: "Let us take care not to be left behind and don't let us be like the chorus at the play which cries 'forward, forward' every two minutes and never stirs a step."[264]

The following is offered as a general framework for adapting to workplace change.

Get Involved

If it becomes apparent that changes are going to be made in your particular work setting, get involved in the planning stage:

- If appropriate, volunteer to serve on a special committee or task force exploring various options.

- Identify issues and problems you would like to see addressed or solved through changes.

- Ask specific questions regarding the nature and implications of proposed changes.

- Articulate clearly your concerns.

- Encourage and support open, honest disclosure of pertinent information to all parties in a timely manner.

- Make an effort to assess proposed changes from the perspective of various stakeholders (e.g., other workers, management, bargaining agent, consumers).

Grieve the Loss

Increasingly, changes within health care settings are having a profound impact on roles, relationships, resources, work schedules, support services, and more. It is important to thoroughly process how changes in your workplace affect you *personally.*

Studies indicate that, even when change results in improvements, there is a perception of loss. Until you acknowledge the personal sense of loss associated with a specific change(s) and allow yourself to "feel the pain" of that loss, you will not be able to adjust to a new set of circumstances, nor will you be able to fully invest yourself in your work.[265] In other words, you must take time to grieve the loss of the way things used to be.

Practice Reframing

As discussed in Chapter 6, self-talk is a key element in stress management. When confronted with planned or unplanned change, every effort should be made to (1) keep an open mind and (2) think positively. As one source notes, "while all change involves loss, it also opens up new opportunities for gain."[266]

Instead of focusing on the possible shortcomings and problems that could arise from a particular change, redirect or "reframe" your thinking to concentrate on the potential benefits to you and others. Psychologist Martin Seligman, for example, encourages individuals to ask themselves: Is there any less destructive way to look at this change? According to Seligman, "looking for evidence of a more positive, less catastrophic view of some change helps you find the energy to take the next steps."[267]

How do you facilitate change in the workplace?

According to Kurt Lewin, change in individuals and organizations is a three-stage process of unfreezing, moving (changing), and refreezing. In the first stage, some stimulus creates an awareness that change is needed. As a result, there is an effort to break down the old way of doing things (i.e., customs, traditions, mores) to facilitate acceptance of something new. In the next stage, a new model of doing things is introduced and a new set of behaviors is demanded for success. In the final stage, the newly acquired behaviors are integrated into existing practices.[268]

The role of the change agent is to assess the readiness of individuals for change, to help frame the need for change, to create the proper motivation, to keep the lines of communication open, to foster effective relationships, and to cultivate a learning environment. Among the traits of a successful change agent are self-confidence, persistence, high energy, commitment, and willingness to take risks.

There is no best strategy for implementing change. According to Hershey and Blanchard, effective change agents adapt their strategies to the demands of the situation.[269] There are numerous studies to identify key factors for facilitating change. For example, Vogt and Murrell contend that people will accept an organizational change if they are:

- Involved in the entire process;

- Asked to give a range of input (knowledge, attitudes, suggestions, feelings, etc.);

- Provided with the reasons for and advantages of the change;

- Informed about all facets of the change;

- Given concrete, specific feedback to identified issues and concerns about the change;

- Respected for their feelings about the change, no matter what their position;

- Asked and given what assistance is needed to deal effectively with the change in their jobs; and

- Recognized appropriately for their specific contributions in implementing the change.[270]

Clearly, the exchange of information is one of the most powerful strategies for combating resistance to change.[271] According to Roe, when sufficient information is shared, it is less likely that employees will make faulty assumptions about planned or unplanned change, and rumors will be curbed.[272] A good workplace communication system will draw from more than one resource to communicate important messages and ensure the flow of two-way communication (i.e., group meetings, newsletters, verbal communication from immediate supervisors, bulletin boards, etc.). Given their numbers and visibility within a health care setting, nurses can play an important role in this process. Roe points out that nurses can have a "powerful influence in their organizations . . . by acting as information links in their health care settings."[273]

Lucie Young Kelly also points out that nurses, because they are "the only health professionals in contact with every facet of the health care system," are in key positions to bring about change.[274] Much has been written, in fact, on the role of nurses as change agents. It is important for nurses to be able to draw from theories of change and related bodies of knowledge (group dynamics, reflective thinking, problem-solving/decision-making processes, etc.) to facilitate desired responses. It is recommended that certain guidelines be used when introducing change to any group in any setting:

1. Identify practical and realistic goals.

2. Set priorities.

3. Reduce any surprises by keeping everyone informed and encouraging two-way communication.

4. Foster dialogue that involves group members in full participation and work toward consensus on the change.

5. Seek a commitment from those involved in the change to listen to each other's contributions and to work to resolve conflict as it arises.

6. Remain responsive to modification at any point during the implementation of the change.

7. Keep the group on target by focusing on the issues and clarifying any problems.[275]

When these guidelines are used in conjunction with integrative problem solving, change becomes more manageable for all parties involved.

PROFESSIONAL SECURITY

Restructuring and work redesign are occurring in every industry. According to Ronni Sandroff, in an article entitled "The Psychology of Change," there are "no safe havens, no stable industries, no occupational ranks in which business as usual still suffices."[276]

Unlike their parents and grandparents, today's workers are likely to change jobs several times during their working lives. In fact, the most recent data indicates that individuals beginning careers in the 1990s will work in 10 or more jobs for five or more employers before retiring.[277]

It is no longer realistic to assume that an employer is going to help guide and develop a career. Nor is it realistic to assume that any specific employment arrangement guarantees a lifetime career. In today's market, all workers, including registered nurses, are being challenged to acquire the skills and knowledge that will allow them to build *career security* out of what may be numerous jobs over a lifetime.

What is being done to address registered nurses' employment security?

In *Job Satisfaction Strategies for Health Care Professionals*, Leebov notes that, over the years, many people chose health care careers because they traditionally offered job security. Given the "turbulent" state of the health care industry, Leebov points out that "life has become very uncomfortable for such security-oriented people."[278]

For many nurses (especially those working in hospitals), job security is a growing concern. Restructuring and redesign activities have led to shifts in practice sites, changes in staffing levels and skill mix, and even layoffs. In 1993, the American Nurses Association (ANA) convened a "nursing summit" to begin to identify strategies to better position nurses for the future. The following year, ANA's governing body expressed its commitment to protecting registered nurse employment security by adopting a special report on "Strategic Directions to Maintain Registered Nurses as the Key Component in Quality Patient Care Today and into the Future."

This report calls for "a multi-faceted strategic initiative . . . to ensure that the professional and economic security of nursing and the quality of patient care are not compromised."[279] It outlines activities in several areas, including data collection, policy discussion with management, education, workplace advocacy and collective bargaining, public relations, litigation, and regulation. Among other things, the association is working to collect scientific data to validate the causal connection between registered nurses' services and quality outcomes. It also has launched a public information campaign to raise consumer consciousness about quality and outcomes as dominant factors in health care cost containment.

While nursing organizations are working collectively to address workplace concerns, individual nurses are being encouraged to scrutinize their career plans. According to ANA, nurses "must plan their careers in much the same way as they watch over their personal finances, health benefits, and pension plans."[280] While staffing patterns are changing in many hospitals, new and different employment opportunities are emerging in a variety of settings, including schools, workplaces, daycare and public health centers, nursing homes, clinics, and hospitals with high-tech intensive care and trauma units. To take advantage of these and other opportunities, nurses must develop "an array of skills, expertise and educational preparation" that equips them with "career mobility options in the shifting job market."[281]

What are the basic keys to successful career planning?

According to one source, planning a career today can be equated to "steering your ship down an unexplored river. The journey requires attentiveness to evolving conditions, the ability to stay on course—and a well-developed taste for surviving by your wits."[282] The following guidelines are intended to prepare you for your "journey."

Be Pro-active

No matter what your level of experience or current situation, career planning should be an ongoing process. According to Barry Grossman and Roy Blitzer, "career advancement comes to those who consciously assess their direction, answer questions about what they want, and then set out to achieve specific objectives . . . ."[283]

Your career plan should be an accurate reflection of who you are and what you want professionally and personally. This necessitates routinely taking stock of your skills, experiences, needs, and preferences.

- Evaluate your nursing skills. Identify your greatest assets, limitations, and any areas needing improvements.

- List your work experiences in nursing and related fields. Identify those functions you enjoy the most and the least, the assignments you have found most challenging and least challenging, and your most significant achievements.

- Identify your needs. Determine which needs are most important at this time.

- List what you value. Pay special attention to what you would like to get from your job besides money.

This self-assessment is the basis for goal setting and for planning a specific course of action to achieve your goals.

Set Specific Career Goals

Career goals should serve as a compass, keeping you on track and ready to make the best decisions regarding the direction of your career.[284] Primary career goals should cover a reasonable period of time. In preparing to develop your goals, consider these questions: Where do you want to be in the development of your career 5 to 10 years from now? What kinds of contributions would you like to make to nursing during this time? What type of nursing role would you like to be ready to assume in 5 to 10 years? What do you hope to accomplish in your personal life in the next 5 to 10 years? (Personal as well as career growth should be taken into account in goal setting.)

In formalizing career goals, keep in mind that your goals should be results oriented, measurable, time bound, realistic, attainable, and significant. You should use action words in phrasing these goals. Verbs such as *achieve, monitor, interpret, describe, organize,* and *direct* give a clear indication of your objectives.

A word of caution, however, is in order. Given the constant changes occurring in society, it is best to focus on the underlying values and beliefs associated with career objectives and to be willing to exercise flexibility in how specific goals are actually achieved. Be open minded to new and different options for attaining key objectives. Do not lock yourself into following a course of action that may become outdated over time.

Explore a Range of Employment Options

Consultant Jill Sherer stresses the importance of "a big-picture orientation" when it comes to identifying employment opportunities.[285] The sites for health care delivery, the nature of practice in any given setting, and caregiver roles and responsibilities will continue to change and evolve. Nurses must learn to look beyond their current employment situation and past experience to potential opportunities in a range of areas, including managed care, ambulatory care, home health, long-term care, business, and consulting. Nurses also must be open to new and innovative approaches to more traditional roles. These tasks are made easier by keeping informed about what is happening within the industry.

To understand the job market, you must recognize how general trends within the industry affect nursing. It is equally important to stay in touch with developments in your locality. For example:

- Keep track of acquisitions and mergers of local facilities.

- Routinely read the health care want ads. They are a ready source of information about major employers; staffing needs; current titles, job descriptions, and qualifications for various positions; and emerging roles.

- Obtain information about major provider chains and systems operating in the area. Pay particular attention to information about their mission statements and long-range plans.

- Become familiar with the employment services available in the community, including career and vocational counselors, job search firms, career placement centers, college referral assistance, and state job services.

Want ads provide a *starting point* for identifying potential employers, types of nursing openings, and job requirements. However, the most effective way to find out about employment opportunities is through personal contacts. Consequently, it is essential that you cultivate a network. (Refer to the separate section "Networking" in this chapter.)

Market Yourself

Today, health care employers are more carefully scrutinizing the contributions an applicant is apt to make to the overall operation of the organization. Given this fact, it is essential that you "portray yourself in a market relevant way."[286]

Whether you are just entering the job market or seeking career advancement, your resume is a key factor. To maximize the effectiveness of this document as a marketing tool, keep the following in mind:

- Be succinct, interesting, and personal.

- Include your name, address and telephone number; objective; special qualifications; work experience; education; accreditation and licenses; professional memberships; relevant volunteer and community activities; and interesting hobbies.

- Describe your work experience in terms of what you have accomplished. Do not simply present a job description.

- Focus on specific information; avoid generalities.

- Select an attractive layout that draws attention to key selling points.

- Omit salary requirements, unless they are requested.

- Omit references. (You should be given the opportunity to discuss your work experience and skills before a prospective employer consults your references.)

- Develop a cover letter that identifies you, offers a brief overview of your most important qualifications, expresses interest in an interview, and requests a response.

- Direct your resume and cover letter to the appropriate person. If you do not have a specific name, call the employer (e.g., the human resources department) and obtain it.

Job interviewing is equally important. It also can be an extremely stressful process. The best way to minimize stress is to be prepared. Try to schedule your interview at a time during the day when you are at your best. Find out as much as possible about the employer and prospective position before the interview. Develop your own set of questions—remember this is also your chance to secure the necessary data to make an informed decision about the job offer.

Practice verbalizing your responses to questions about your strengths and weaknesses, work experiences, nursing philosophy, career goals, and the reasons you believe you are equipped for the position you are seeking. The importance of first impressions cannot be overstated. During the interview:

- Be enthusiastic.

- Keep your responses brief and to the point.

- Maintain eye contact with your interviewer.

- Downplay any weaknesses by presenting them as areas you are trying to improve.

- Limit negative comments about current or previous employment situations.

- Refrain from bringing up the issue of salary early in the interview.

- Arrange for a follow-up—ask who is to call or write whom and when.

Immediately after the interview, write a note to the primary interviewer expressing your appreciation for the opportunity to discuss your interest in the position.

Continue to Refine Your Skills

A career plan consists of both short- and long-term goals. The short-term goals should be aimed at securing the necessary expertise and experience to achieve primary (long-term) career goals. Consequently, it is important to consider questions such as the following: In what areas will you need to become more proficient or experienced to seek more challenging roles? Do you need to pursue an advanced degree? What type of continuing education opportunities are apt to be most beneficial? Would it be advantageous to seek certification in your area of interest? Should you consider pursuing research and/or writing in nursing? Are there certain journals and other publications you should be reviewing on a regular basis?[287]

In addition to maintaining clinical competency, it is increasingly important to continue to refine your "people skills." According to Robert Bolton, 80% of the people who fail at work do so because they do not relate well to other people.[288] Considerable space in this book has been devoted to discussing skills in such important areas as team-building, group decision making, problem solving, values clarification, assertion, and conflict resolution. There is, however, one remaining dimension of people skills worth mentioning: negotiations.

Webster defines negotiation as "a conferring, discussing, or bargaining to reach an agreement."[289] According to Manion, "in organizations today, skill at negotiation techniques is essential to success."[290] Obviously, the negotiation process draws from many of the same theories and principles applied to decision making, problem solving, and conflict resolution. (Refer to Chapters 5 and 7.)

The methods used in negotiations are the same regardless of the circumstances or the issues being addressed. To ensure successful negotiations, keep the following basic points in mind:

- Areas of common agreement rather than controversial matter should be the starting point for discussions.

- Every attempt should be made to avoid offering a choice between something and nothing. Offering a choice between alternatives may ease the burden of a weighty decision and also avoid the appearance of a forced choice.

- Discussions should be kept problem-oriented rather than personality-oriented.

- By far the most fruitful atmosphere for reaching sound agreements is the recognition by both parties of mutual interest in solving problems of common concerns.

- The greater the degree of objectivity that can be developed, the more constructive the relationship.[291]

When using your negotiations skills:

- Know precisely what you want to accomplish.

- Take sufficient time to gather the necessary facts and relevant information and to check out basic assumptions.

- Be prepared to take risks.

- Negotiate in good faith.

- Put yourself in the other person's shoes.

- Learn to say *yes, no* and *why,* and *stop.* According to experts the use of "why" is one of the best negotiation tactics.

- Don't argue or disagree, seek more information.

- Ask open-ended questions.

- Don't lose your temper or your sense of humor.

- Reach closure.

NETWORKING

As stated earlier, networking is a key element in career development. A network is a collection of individuals who serve as a source of support, information, and guidance. When properly cultivated, networking can give you "a sense of professional community, of being able to discuss plans, thoughts, and feelings with a supportive peer group."[292]

What does networking involve?

Networking is the process of identifying and accessing contacts. An effective network draws from a variety of sources, including employers and supervisors; co-workers; instructors and fellow students; fellow members of civic, religious, and social groups; and family, friends, and neighbors. It is very important to continually expand your network. Anne Baber and Lynne Waymon recommend looking both inside the workplace and outside.[293] At work, networking should occur with "people within your own work group, people below your level, people at your own level, and people one or more levels up."[294] Baber and Waymon also recommend networking outside the workplace with people in the same industry, people in similar jobs, people in jobs "you would like to move to," and people "whose perspective is totally different from yours."[295]

Any number of activities can be used to expand your number of contacts. For example, membership in organizations; attendance at professional workshops, seminars, conventions, and special meetings; volunteer work; and involvement in political action offer valuable opportunities to connect with a broad range of people.

To take full advantage of these and other opportunities, it is important to give careful consideration to how networking can help further your career goals. It is also important to master the art of small talk. As Baber and Waymon point out, "at the heart of networking is the ability to small talk."[296] In *Great Connections, Small*

Talk and Networking for Businesspeople, Baber and Waymon provide useful tips and advice on communication strategies for networking purposes.

By giving careful thought to the potential benefits of networking, you begin to develop an agenda. According to Baber and Waymon, having an agenda is both energizing and empowering.[297] Once contacts have been identified, it is important to devote the necessary time and energy to maintaining an effective network.

- Keep a special file of the names, addresses, and phone numbers of those individuals in your network.

- To help remember each contact, jot down key phrases on the backs of their business cards.

- Use a calendar to keep track of the frequency of your contacts and the nature of each encounter/meeting.

- Write personal notes after meetings, workshops, and social events, expressing appreciation for a suggestion or the identification of a potential contact.

- Periodically send contacts articles and other information on subjects that you think will interest them.

Networking is a reciprocal process. It is equally important that you give careful thought to how you can be of assistance to others. Helping others whenever possible also will strengthen your own network.

What is the role of a mentor?

Networking also can lead to a mentoring relationship. A mentor is defined as "a more experienced career role model who guides, coaches, and advises the less seasoned person" (also referred to as a novice or protege).[298] While mentoring is not essential to career success, it does hold a number of advantages.

Connie Vance describes a mentor as a "visionary" who is able to see an individual's true potential—potential of which the individual may be unaware.[299] Hamilton and Kiefer point out that "a mentor is one who takes a deep personal interest in you and your career."[300] Judith Leavitt and Camille Barry contend that true mentoring involves a relationship in which "there is an emotional investment and commitment to the development of the protege."[301] According to Leavitt and Barry, this commitment includes a willingness on the mentor's part to use personal power and influence on the protege's behalf.[302]

A mentor assumes a variety of roles, including teacher-coach, career counselor, problem solver, challenger, sounding board, motivator, door opener, and supporter. Research suggests that mentoring relationships in the workplace can actually lead to improvement in morale, reduction in stress, and greater productivity.[303]

What are the characteristics of a highly effective mentor?

In a survey of nursing service executives, Suzanne Holloran discovered four recurring themes. Nurses who consistently rated their mentors high reported the following behaviors/functions: (1) giving encouragement and recognizing potential, (2) giving opportunities and responsibilities, (3) providing inspiration and a role model, and (4) helping with career moves.[304]

The responsibility for finding a mentor rests with the protege or novice. If you are searching for a mentor, keep the following questions in mind:

- Is this individual someone I admire and trust?

- Is this individual highly knowledgeable in my area of interest?

- Does this individual demonstrate a high level of professional enthusiasm?

- Can this individual help me attain my career goals?

- Is this individual likely to have the time and be willing to make a commitment to a nurturing relationship?

- Does this individual possess good communication skills?

- Will this individual challenge me to expand my thinking by exposing me to new ideas, concepts, and possibilities?

- Can this individual teach me important technical, interpersonal, political, and/or professional skills?

- Will this individual offer emotional encouragement and reassurance?

By slightly modifying these questions, you also can assess your ability to assume the role of a mentor.

What are the advantages of organizational memberships?

One of the easiest and most obvious ways to network is to join an organization. Today, there are many nursing and health-related organizations to meet a wide range of needs and interests. (A directory of organizations appears each year in the *AJN.*)

The American Nurses Association, for example, has been addressing the issues and concerns of nurses since 1896. Since 1982, ANA has been a federation of 53 state nurses associations (SNAs), which include 50 states, the District of Columbia, Guam, and the Virgin Islands. In addition to valuable contacts, ANA/SNA affiliation offers opportunities for professional development and leadership training, a vehicle for political action, collective bargaining representation and workplace advocacy, information and data resources, and much more. Special membership benefits and services range from group insurance plans and financial programs to publications and other products.

The best way to become familiar with a particular organization(s) is to gather as much information as possible. This information should include bylaws, mission statement, and long- and short-term goals; annual reports and issues of the organization's official publication; list of key officers; and membership packet. The most valuable information, however, comes from individual members. It is important to ask the questions: Why did you decide to get involved in this organization? and How have you benefitted professionally and personally from membership in this organization?

In weighing the merits of membership in various nursing and/or health-related organizations, consider the following factors:

- How does membership in this particular organization help meet my career goals?

- What can I hope to accomplishment through involvement in this organization?

- How might I put my particular skills and knowledge to use in this organization?

- What are the basic demographics of the organization?

- To what extent do members have input into the various levels of the organization?

- What types of professional issues and concerns are addressed within the organization?

- Does the organization appear to be attuned to the changing environment of the health care industry? Is the organization taking the necessary steps to maintain its relevancy?

- To what degree, if any, does the organization deal with workplace issues?

Similar questions also can be asked about potential membership in other types of organizations and special interest groups.

No matter what organization(s) you join, the greatest benefits will be derived from active participation. Do not wait for an invitation to serve on a committee or run for office—volunteer! The more involved you are in an organization, the more opportunity you will have to grow and develop professionally and personally.

SUMMARY

In preparing for tomorrow, nurses must become "change-skilled." They must learn to anticipate changes in the making. They must approach traditional roles and responsibilities in new and creative ways. Most importantly, they must be willing to assume greater responsibility for shaping their own careers. By developing a sound career plan, refining skills and knowledge, and cultivating a professional network, nurses will be able to take full advantage of a wide range of employment opportunities.

CONCLUSION

The health care industry and nursing, in particular, are a microcosm of what is happening in society. Both the industry at large and the local workplace are responding to economic, social, and political forces that have necessitated a restructuring of the health care system. Increased demand for health care and changes in the organization, financing, and delivery of services pose both challenges and opportunities for nurses. It is imperative for nurses to become more sophisticated about survival and growth in an industry playing under new ground rules. In short, this means that nurses must become more business-minded professionals, more effective leaders in the workplace, and more discerning employees.

What are the basic characteristics of these roles?

A business-minded professional:

- Stays informed of trends influencing the industry and the nursing profession.

- Understands the economic forces operating in the health care system.

- Uses data to document the value of nursing services, to document the importance of nurse staffing levels, and skills mix, etc.

- Is able to translate consumer needs and budget considerations into programs that ensure cost-effective, quality care.

- Learns to anticipate and manage change.

- Understands the implications of workplace reorganization, restructuring, and redesign.

- Is familiar with organizational schemes and management practices.

- Participates in workplace decision making.

- Is aware of the factors contributing to a work environment supportive of quality controls.

- Draws upon a well-developed network for support, guidance, and information.

- Assumes greater responsibility for career development.

An effective workplace leader:

- Lays the groundwork for effective interaction with others by enhancing self-understanding.

- Implements a self-care plan, which includes strategies for stress management.

- Cultivates effective communication skills, especially listening skills.

- Is able to assess work group culture and work group climate.

- Possesses basic knowledge about group development and group dynamics.

- Is sensitive to diversity in the workforce.

- Practices assertive communication.

- Is open to resolving conflicts.

- Facilitates integrative problem solving.

A discerning employee:

- Understands basic workplace laws and regulations.

- Stays apprised of legislative, legal, and agency activities having an impact on employment rights and protections.

- Is knowledgeable about the employer and terms and conditions of employment.

- Keeps track of trends in compensation practices, employee assistance, and workplace policies and benefits.

- Maintains current information about the labor market.

- Presses for workplace policies, programs, and services aimed at minimizing stressful working conditions.

- Makes sure there are appropriate mechanisms in place to resolve workplace problems (e.g., grievance handling).

- Fosters healthy working relationships through assertiveness.

- Seeks strategies for addressing such complex issues as sexual harassment and workplace violence.

What should every nurse know about workplace survival?

Novice and experienced nurses alike must cultivate a unique set of skills. Beyond continually expanding clinical expertise, nurses must learn to apply knowledge and skills from a variety of fields, including economics, labor law, human resources, and the behavioral sciences. In so doing, they will experience a greater sense of control in the workplace.

Appendix

Sources of Information on Employment Rights and Protections

Clearly, nurses need to stay apprised of legislative, legal, and agency activity influencing workplace laws and regulations. Consequently, awareness of the wide variety of resources from which to draw current information is important. The following is a brief overview of some potential sources.

- Most agencies with enforcement or administrative responsibilities for *federal laws* print information pamphlets. Free copies of these materials are generally available from the agency upon request.

- Various private concerns also attempt to keep current with the frequent changes in the laws of the workplace. For example, the Bureau of National Affairs, Inc. (BNA), based in Washington, DC, is one of several private companies providing *up-to-date information on federal legislation*. BNA periodically updates its publication, *The Law of the Workplace: Rights of Employers and Employees*. Buraff Publications compiles a biweekly newsletter, *AIDS Policy & Law*, which contains the *latest information on legislation, regulation, and litigation concerning AIDS*.

- The Office of the Federal Register prepares *The United States Government Manual*. It is regarded as the official handbook of the federal government. The manual provides *comprehensive information on the agencies of the legislative, judicial, and executive branches*. It also includes information on quasiofficial agencies; international organizations in which the United States participates; and boards, commissions, and committees.

- The *Federal Register* is issued each federal working day. It provides a system for publishing Presidential documents, regulatory documents with general applicability and legal effect, proposed rules, notices, and documents required to be published by statutes. The *Federal Register* is, for example, one of the best sources of *information on OSHA standards*. It is available in many public libraries.

115

- An excellent source of *information on state legislation* is the *Monthly Labor Review*, a publication of the U.S. Department of Labor, which is available in most libraries. Its annual January issue contains a complete summary of the workplace laws enacted by state legislatures in the preceding year.

- The Chamber of Commerce of the United States, located in Washington, DC, routinely compiles an *analysis of workers' compensation laws.*

- Additional sources of assistance and information are usually available through community-based organizations that have information, referral, counseling, or legal services. The local bar association or the state commission on women, for example, may be able to provide information on these sources.

The U.S. Department of Labor (DOL) is a *primary source of workplace information.* The DOL is responsible for protecting the wages, health and safety, employment, and pension rights of working people; promoting equal opportunity employment; administering job training, unemployment insurance, and workers' compensation programs; strengthening collective bargaining; and publishing labor and economic statistics. The following are a few of the DOL agencies:

Bureau of Labor Statistics

This agency collects, analyzes, and publishes information about employment, unemployment, occupational outlook, wages and salaries, working hours, industrial relations, prices, productivity, economic growth, and job safety and health.

Employment and Training Administration

This agency administers training programs such as the Job Training Partnership Act. It operates state employment and service offices to help people find jobs. The agency also is responsible for the unemployment insurance system, which provides benefits to workers who lose their jobs.

Employment Standards Administration

This agency enforces labor standards laws including minimum wage, overtime pay, and child labor provisions of the Fair Labor Standards Act. It also administers equal employment opportunity requirements for federal contractors and subcontractors, and workers' compensation programs for federal employees.

Occupational Safety and Health Administration

This agency enforces the Occupational Safety and Health Act. It issues workplace safety and health standards, conducts inspections to assure that standards are followed, and promotes safety training, education, consultation, cooperative efforts, and voluntary initiatives.

Office of the American Workplace

This agency was established under the Clinton Administration to promote labor-management cooperation and high performance work practices. Its role is to assist employers, employees, and labor organizations in improving the quality of American jobs and the long-term performance of U.S. firms. The agency includes offices that deal with work and technology policy, labor-management programs, and labor-management standards.

Pension and Welfare Benefits Administration

This agency is responsible for standards designed to protect the assets of workers participating in private pension and benefit plans. It enforces provisions of the Employee Retirement Income Security Act.

Women's Bureau

This agency was established exclusively to improve employment opportunities for women. Numerous publications have been produced by the bureau to further this goal, including *A Working Woman's Guide to Her Job Rights* and *Work and Family Resource Kit.*

Finally, the following is a partial resource list of who to contact regarding specific concerns and/or interests:

Discrimination

- Race, color, religion, sex, national origin, age, sex (as related to wages), disability (under Title I of the Americans with Disabilities Act)

  U.S. Equal Employment Opportunity Commission (EEOC)
  1801 L Street, NW
  Washington, DC 20507
  (202) 663-4900

  EEOC field offices
  (800) USA-EEOC

- Discrimination by federal contractors (including race, color, religion, sex, national origin, disability)

  Office of Federal Contract Compliance Programs (OFCCP)
  Employment Standards Administration
  U.S. Department of Labor
  200 Constitution Avenue, NW
  Washington, DC 20210
  (202) 523-9368

  OFCCP regional or district offices listed in the telephone directory under U.S. Government, Department of Labor

- Discrimination in programs or activities receiving federal financial assistance

  Specific federal agencies providing assistance

Fair Labor Standards

  U.S. Department of Labor
  Employment Standards Administration
  Wage and Hour Division
  200 Constitution Avenue, NW
  Washington, DC 20210
  (202) 219-8305

  Local offices of the Wage and Hour Division are listed in the telephone directory under U.S. Government, Department of Labor, Employment Standards Administration

Unfair Labor Standards

- Private Sector Employees

   National Labor Relations Board (NLRB)
   1099 Fourteenth Street, NW
   Washington, DC 20570
   (202) 273-1991

   NLRB's 34 regional offices are listed in the telephone directory under U.S. Government, National Labor Relations Board

- State Employees

   Individual state labor relations boards

- Federal Employees

   Federal Labor Relations Authority (FLRA)
   607 Fourteenth Street, NW
   Washington, DC 20424-0001
   (202) 482-6550

   Regional offices are listed in the telephone directory under U.S. Government, Federal Labor Relations Authority

Job Safety and Health Protection

Occupational Safety and Health Administration
U.S. Department of Labor
200 Constitution Avenue, NW
Washington, DC 20210
(202) 219-8151

OSHA Regional Offices

Atlanta, GA	(404) 347-3573	Kansas City, MO	(816) 426-5861
Boston, MA	(617) 565-7164	New York City, NY	(212) 337-2378
Chicago, IL	(312) 353-2220	Philadelphia, PA	(215) 596-1201
Dallas, TX	(214) 767-4731	San Francisco, CA	(415) 744-6670
Denver, CO	(303) 844-3061	Seattle, WA	(206) 442-5930

State Occupational Safety and Health Agencies

Family-Oriented Employment Policies

The Women's Bureau has established a toll-free number (800-827-5335) to a computerized data base (CHOICES), with information for employers interested in child care and other family-oriented employment policies.

HIV/AIDS Information

National AIDS Information Clearinghouse (NAIC)
P.O. Box 6003
Rockville, MD 20850
(800) 458-5231; (301) 762-5111

Centers for Disease Control and Prevention

National AIDS Hotline
(800) 342-AIDS (English); (800) 344-SIDA (Spanish)

CDC's Business Responds to AIDS Resource Service
(800) 458-5231

National Leadership Coalition on AIDS

1730 M Street, Suite 703
Washington, DC 20036
(202) 429-0930

REFERENCES

1. Barbara J. Stevens, *The Nurse as Executive* (Rockville, MD: Aspen Publishers, 1985), 167.
2. Nathan Kaufman, "Eight Guidelines for Developing a Strategy for the '90s," *Hospitals & Health Networks* 68, No. 6 (March 20, 1994), 78.
3. Catherine D. Buckley and Diane Walker, *Harmony: Professional Renewal for Nurses* (Chicago, IL: American Hospital Publishing, 1989), 113.
4. Alden T. Solovy, "Retooling the Hospital: Moving into the Second Phase," *Hospitals* 67, No. 5 (March 5, 1993), 18.
5. Ibid.
6. "Strategic Directions to Maintain Registered Nurses as the Key Component in Quality Patient Care Today and into the Future," *Summary of Proceedings, 1994 ANA House of Delegates*, 54. (Washington, DC: American Nurses Association).
7. Emily Friedman, "Health Care's Changing Face: The Demographics of the 21st Century," *Hospitals* 65, No. 7 (April 5, 1991), 37.
8. Ibid., 40.
9. Barbara Gastel, "Hospitals and Hospitals: Evolving Together," *Hospitals* 67, No. 10 (May 20, 1993), 64.
10. Howard Anderson, "Hospitals Seek New Ways to Integrate Health Care," *Hospitals* 66, No. 7 (April 5, 1992), 27.
11. Ibid., 28.
12. Ibid., 30.
13. Clare Hastings, Sharon O'Keefe, and Janet Buckley, "Professional Practice Partnerships: A New Approach to Creating High Performance Nursing Organizations," *Nursing Administration Quarterly* 17, No. 1 (Fall 1992), 45.
14. James W. Hunt, *The Law of the Workplace: Rights of Employers and Employees* (Washington, DC: The Bureau of National Affairs, Inc., 1988), v.
15. Ibid.
16. "Drugs in the Workplace: Recent Regulatory Developments," *Labor Relations Week*, 12 April 1989, 339.
17. "ANA Guards Workers' Rights to Workplace Privacy," *The American Nurse* 25, No. 8 (September 1993), 12.
18. Ibid.
19. American Nurses Association, *Guidelines on Reporting Incompetent, Unethical or Illegal Practices* (Washington, DC: the Association, 1994), 12.
20. "Supreme Court Issues Fragmented Ruling on Free Speech Rights of Public Employees," *Government Employee Relations Report* 32, No. 1568 (June 7, 1994), 20.
21. Ibid.
22. American Nurses Association, *How Do You Know . . . If Your Paycheck Is Correct?* (Washington, DC: the Association, 1994), 1–2.
23. Ibid., 2.
24. Ibid.
25. "New Tax Reform Legislation Could Slow Benefit Plan Growth," *E&GW Update* 5, No. 8 (December 12, 1986), 1.

26. "American Nurses Association Pension Portability/Reform Project," *Summary of Proceedings, 1993 ANA House of Delegates*, 29. (Washington, DC: American Nurses Association).
27. Joni Ketter, "Surviving Layoffs," *The American Nurse* 26, No. 7 (July/August 1994), 25.
28. "WARN Amendments Give Added Protection to Nurses," *The American Nurse* 26, No. 7 (July/August 1994), 25.
29. Hunt, *Law of the Workplace*, 65.
30. "Labor Secretary, Aging Advocates Warn Congress of Need to Adjust to Needs of Older Workforce," *Daily Labor Report*, 15 September 1988, A-1.
31. The Bureau of National Affairs, Inc., *Preventing Sexual Harassment, A Fact Sheet for Employees* (Rockville, MD: BNA Books, 1992), 2.
32. Ibid.
33. Rosalee M. McNamara, "Court Decision Narrowed Outlines of Harassment," *The Kansas City Star*, 22 March 1994, D-18.
34. American Nurses Association, *Position Statement on Sexual Harassment*, 1993, 3.
35. "Court Rules Title VII Permits More Favorable Pregnancy Benefits," *Daily Labor Report*, 28 September 1989, A-1.
36. Ibid.
37. "Family and Medical Leave Act Regulations," *Union Labor Report* 47, No. 23 (June 10, 1993), 5.
38. Ibid.
39. American Nurses Association, *Fact Sheet on the Family and Medical Leave Act (FMLA) of 1993*, 5 April 1993, 1.
40. "Understanding the Americans with Disabilities Act, A Fact Sheet for Employees," *Union Labor Report* 47, No. 14 (April 8, 1993), 4.
41. Ibid.
42. "OSHA Reform Legislation," *Capital Update* 12, No. 6 (April 1, 1994), 2.
43. "Hazard Communication/Right-to-Know," Health and Safety Issues in the Healthcare Workplace, ANA Communication Workshop for Local Bargaining Unit Leaders, July 1993, 1.
44. Randy Rabinowitz, *Is Your Job Making You Sick? A CLUW Handbook on Workplace Hazards* (New York: Coalition of Labor Union Women, 1992), 4.
45. Karen Worthington, "Workplace Hazards: The Effect on Nurses as Women," *The American Nurse* 26, No. 2 (February 1994), 15.
46. Ibid.
47. American Nurses Association, *Nursing and HIV/AIDS* (Washington, DC: American Nurses Publishing, 1994), 93.
48. Ibid., 18.
49. "Workers' Compensation Issues Related to Bloodborne Diseases," *Report to ANA's Commission on Economic and Professional Security*, February 1993, 2.
50. Lyndia Flanagan, "The Hospital Industry: A Decade of Change," *E&GW Update* 11, No. 1 (March 1993), 27.
51. "TB-Related Inspections," *Organizing* 3, No. 3 (December 1993), 9–10.
52. "OSHA Chief: A New Voice on Safety—Joseph A. Dear," *Hospitals & Health Networks* 68, No. 13 (July 5, 1994), 55.
53. Buckley and Walker, *Harmony: Professional Renewal for Nurses*, 115.
54. Howard S. Rowland and Beatrice L. Rowland, *Hospital Administration Handbook* (Rockville, MD: Aspen Systems Corporation, 1984), 455.
55. Stevens, *The Nurse as Executive*, 372–374.
56. Lynda Nauright, "Toward a Comprehensive Personnel System: Performance Appraisal, Part IV," *Nursing Management* 18, No. 8 (August 1987), 68.
57. Stevens, *The Nurse as Executive*, 375.

58. American Nurses Association, *Liability Prevention & You, What Nurses & Employers Need to Know* (Washington, DC: the Association, 1992), 3.

59. Rowland and Rowland, *Hospital Administration Handbook*, 688–689.

60. "Employment Benefits," *E&GW Update* 8, No. 1 (February 23, 1990), 3.

61. U.S. Department of Labor, Office of the Secretary, Women's Bureau, *Work and Family Resource Kit* (Washington, DC: U.S. Office, 1989), 2.

62. Ibid., 3–5.

63. "Policies and Benefits Supportive of Working Parents," *E&GW Update* 4, No. 10 (October 17, 1986), 4–6.

64. "Eldercare Will Become Employee Benefit of the 1990s," *E&GW Update* 4, No. 7 (July 18, 1986), 7.

65. "Policies and Benefits Supportive of Working Parents," 7.

66. Ibid.

67. Karen S. Wulff, "Flextime and Self-Scheduling Benefits and Difficulties" in *Current Issues in Nursing*, eds. Joanne McCloskey and Helen K. Grace (St. Louis: Mosby-Year Book, Inc., 1994), 262.

68. U.S. Department of Labor, 3.

69. "Policies and Benefits Supportive of Working Parents," 14.

70. BNA PLUS Research, "Nontraditional Benefits for the Workforce of 2000" in *The Future of Work & Family: Shaping Programs for the 21st Century, Special Report #34* (Washington, DC, BNA, 1990), 29–30.

71. Ketter, "Surviving Layoffs," 25.

72. Ibid.

73. American Nurses Association, "Surviving Layoffs—Severance Packages and Outplacement Services" in *Health Care Layoffs: Developing A Strategic Plan from the State Nurses Association Perspective*, H-2. (Washington, DC: American Nurses Association).

74. Ibid.

75. American Nurses Association, *Local Unit Handbook, A Basic Resource for SNA Bargaining Units* (Washington, DC: the Association, 1993), 86.

76. American Nurses Association, *Guidelines on Reporting Incompetent, Unethical or Illegal Practices*, 5.

77. Ibid., 8.

78. Ibid., 8–9.

79. Maureen Cushing, "Accepting or Rejecting an Assignment, Part 2: Strategies for Problem Solving," *American Journal of Nursing* 88, No. 12 (December 1988), 1635–1636.

80. Ibid., 1636.

81. Catherine P. Murphy and Howard Hunter, *Ethical Problems in the Nurse-Patient Relationship* (Newton, MA: Allyn & Bacon, 1983), 1.

82. Joni Ketter, "ANA: Protecting Nurses and Patient Care in the Face of Restructuring," *The American Nurse* 26, No. 5 (May 1994), 1.

83. Flanagan, "The Hospital Industry," 5.

84. Joni Ketter, "When 1+1=1, How 'Merger Mania' Is Impacting Nurses Across America," *The American Nurse* 26, No. 7 (July/August 1994), 24.

85. Terry G. Minnen, Elizabeth Burger, Adrienne Ames, Marilyn Dubree, Wendy L. Baker, and Judy Spinella, "Sustaining Work Redesign Innovations Through Shared Governance," *Journal of Nursing Administration* 23, No. 7/8 (July/August), 35.

86. "What Restructuring May Mean to Nurses," *The American Nurse* 26, No. 5 (May 1994), 14.

87. Rhonda Bergman, "Reengineering Health Care," *Hospitals & Health Networks* 68, No. 3 (February 5, 1994), 28.

88. Ibid., 28, 30.

89. Ibid., 28.
90. Jacqueline Dienemann, ed., *C.Q.I., Continuous Quality Improvement in Nursing* (Washington, DC: American Nurses Publishing, 1992), 12.
91. Jacqueline Dienemann, "Share Ideas to Speed CQI Success," *The American Nurse* 25, No. 1 (January 1993), 4.
92. American Nurses Association, "ADVISORY: Total Quality Management (TQM), Continuous Quality Improvement (CQI), Joint Governance," 1994, 2.
93. Joseph R. Jablonski, *Implementing TQM—Competing in the Nineties Through Total Quality Management* (Albuquerque, NM: Technical Management Consortium, 1992), 41.
94. Ibid., 44–49.
95. Eleanor Davidson, "Communicating With A Diverse Workforce," *Supervisory Management* 36, No. 12 (December 1991), 1.
96. Flanagan, "The Hospital Industry" 24.
97. Christine Lajkowicz, "Teaching Cultural Diversity for the Workplace," *Journal of Nursing Education* 32, No. 5 (May 1993), 235.
98. Ibid.
99. Ibid.
100. Mildred Roberson, "Defining Cultural and Ethnic Differences to Adapt to a Changing Patient Population," *The American Nurse* 25, No. 8 (September 1993), 6.
101. Ibid.
102. "Ways to Develop Your Cultural Sensitivity," *The American Nurse* 25, No. 8 (September 1993), 16.
103. Divina Grossman, "Enhancing Your Cultural Competence," *AJN 94*, No. 7 (July 1994), 62.
104. Alexander Hamilton Institute, *What Every Manager Must Know To Prevent Sexual Harassment* (Maywood, NJ: the Institute, 1991), 9.
105. American Nurses Association, *Position Statement on Sexual Harassment*, 3.
106. Ibid.
107. "A Self-Evaluation of Sexual Harassment Policies—Does Your Company's Policy Do The Job?" *Fair Employment* Practices, 2 March 1992, 2–3.
108. American Nurses Association, *Sexual Harassment—It's Against the Law* (Washington, DC: the Association, 1993), 2.
109. "Nurses at Greatest Risk for Workplace Violence Due to Gang Activity and Drugs, Report Says," ANA News Release, March 24, 1993, 1.
110. Ibid.
111. Karen Worthington, "Taking Action Against Violence in the Workplace," *The American Nurse* 25, No. 6 (June 1993), 12.
112. Jane Meier Hamilton and Marcy E. Kiefer, *Survival Skills for the New Nurse* (Philadelphia: J. B. Lippincott, 1986), 82.
113. Kenneth Blanchard, Donald Carew, and Eunice Parisi-Carew, *The One-Minute Manager Builds High Performing Teams* (New York: William Morrow and Company, Inc., 1990), 6.
114. Russell L. Ackoff, "The Circular Organization: An Update," *Academy of Management Executive*, February 1989, 7.
115. Judith F. Vogt and Kenneth L. Murrell, *Empowerment In Organizations, How To Spark Exceptional Performance* (San Diego, CA: University Associates, Inc., 1990), 8.
116. Ibid.
117. Jim Hamilton, "Toppling the Power of the Pyramid," *Hospitals* 68, No. 1 (January 5, 1993), 41.
118. Edward E. Lawler III, *High Involvement Management* (San Francisco: Jossey-Bass Publishers, 1988), 22–23.

119. Ibid., 28.
120. Minnen et al., "Sustaining Work Redesign Innovations," 37.
121. Ibid.
122. Meridean L. Maas and Janet P. Specht, "Shared Governance in Nursing—What Is Shared, Who Governs, and Who Benefits" in *Current Issues in Nursing*, eds. Joanne McCloskey and Helen K. Grace (St. Louis: Mosby-Year Book, Inc., 1994), 400.
123. Ibid.
124. Ibid., 401.
125. Tim Porter-O'Grady, "Transformational Leadership in an Age of Chaos," *Nursing Administration Quarterly* 17, No. 1 (Fall 1992), 18–19.
126. Ibid., 21.
127. Paul Hershey and Kenneth H. Blanchard, *Management of Organizational Behavior, Utilizing Human Resources* (Englewood Cliffs, NJ: Prentice-Hall, 1988), 5.
128. Ibid.
129. Ibid., 143.
130. Ibid., 170.
131. Ibid., 173.
132. Ibid., 182.
133. Laura Mae Douglass, *The Effective Nurse—Leader and Manager* (St. Louis: C. V. Mosby, 1984), 4–5.
134. Hamilton and Kiefer, *Survival Skills*, 84.
135. Harriet Van Ess Coeling and Lillian M. Simms, "Facilitating Innovation at the Nursing Unit Level Through Cultural Assessment, Part I, How To Keep Management Ideas from Falling on Deaf Ears," *Journal of Nursing Administration* 23, No. 4 (April 1993), 48.
136. Ibid., 49.
137. Dominick L. Flarey, "The Social Climate Scale, A Tool for Organizational Change and Development," *Journal of Nursing Administration* 21, No. 4, 37.
138. Ibid.
139. Coeling and Simms, "Facilitating Innovation," 51.
140. Blanchard, Carew, and Parisi-Carew, *The One-Minute Manager*, 32.
141. Irwin D. Yalom, *The Theory and Practice of Group Psychotherapy* (New York: Basic Books, 1985), 301–310.
142. Blanchard, Carew, and Parisi-Carew, *The One-Minute Manager*, 39.
143. Yalom, *The Theory and Practice of Group Psychotherapy*, 301–310.
144. Blanchard, Carew, and Parisi-Carew, *The One-Minute Manager*, 47.
145. Carl E. Larson and Frank M. J. LaFasto, *TeamWork—What Must Go Right/What Can Go Wrong* (New York: Sage Publications, 1989), 26.
146. Blanchard, Carew, and Parisi-Carew, *The One-Minute Manager*, 20.
147. Louis V. Imundo, "Blueprint for a Successful Team," *Supervisory Management*, May 1992, 2–3.
148. Bill D. Schul, *How To Be An Effective Group Leader* (Chicago: Nelson-Hall, 1975), 99.
149. John Dewey, *How We Think* (Boston: D. C. Health & Company, 1963), 1–20.
150. Susan C. Roe, "Conflict Management and Change" in *Management Concepts for the New Nurse*, ed. Katherine W. Vestal (Philadelphia: J. B. Lippincott, 1987), 93.
151. Peggy S. Williams, "Physical Fitness for Committees: Getting on Track," *Association Management* 41, No. 6 (June 1989), 105–111.
152. Barbara A. Norton and Anna M. Miller, *Skills for Professional Nursing Practice* (Norwalk, CT: Appleton-Century-Crofts, 1986), 78.
153. Rowland and Rowland, *Hospital Administration Handbook*, 449.
154. Emily E. M. Smythe, *Surviving Nursing* (Menlo Park, CA: Addision-Wesley, 1984), 59.
155. Dennis T. Jaffe and Cynthia D. Scott, *From Burnout to Balance, A Workbook for Peak Performance and Self-Renewal* (New York: McGraw-Hill Book Company, 1984), 36.

156. Ronald G. Nathan, Thomas E. Staats, and Paul J. Rosch, *The Doctors' Guide to Instant Stress Relief* (New York: Ballantine Books, 1987), 11.

157. Ibid., 11–12.

158. Jaffe and Scott, *From Burnout to Balance*, 3.

159. Douglass, *The Effective Nurse*, 181.

160. Glynis M. Breakwell, "Are You Stressed Out?" *American Journal of Nursing* 90, No. 8 (August 1990), 31, 33.

161. J. Dionne-Proulx and R. Pepin, "Stress Management in the Nursing Profession," *Journal of Nursing Management* 1 (1993), 75.

162. Ibid.

163. "Women Face More Hazards in Workplace Than Ever Before, BNA Report Says," *Labor Relations Week*, 18 January 1989, 49.

164. Ibid., 3.

165. Hamilton and Kiefer, *Survival Skills*, 195.

166. Ayala Pines and Elliot Aronson, *Career Burnout Causes & Cures* (New York: The Free Press, 1988), 83.

167. Diana Lynn Gallagher, "Is Stress Ripping Nurses Apart?" *Imprint* 36, No. 2 (April/May 1989), 59.

168. Ibid.

169. Terrance L. Albrecht, "What Job Stress Means for the Staff Nurse," *Nursing Administration Quarterly* 7, No. 1 (Fall 1982), 3.

170. Ibid., 2.

171. Ibid., 1–10.

172. Buckley and Walker, *Harmony: Professional Renewal for Nurses*, 82.

173. Smythe, *Surviving Nursing*, 59.

174. Hans Selye, *The Stress of Life* (New York: McGraw, 1976), 443.

175. Nathan et al., *Instant Stress Relief*, 47.

176. Jaffe and Scott, *From Burnout to Balance*, 44–45.

177. Jeanne M. Aurelio, "An Organizational Culture That Optimizes Stress: Acceptable Stress in Nursing," *Nursing Administration Quarterly* 18, No. 1 (Fall 1993), 1.

178. Buckley and Walker, *Harmony: Professional Renewal for Nurses*, 58.

179. Ibid.

180. Jaffe and Scott, *From Burnout to Balance*, 50.

181. Smythe, *Surviving Nursing*, 198.

182. Buckley and Walker, *Harmony: Professional Renewal for Nurses*, 60.

183. Nathan et al., *Instant Stress Relief*, 109.

184. Nathan et al., *Instant Stress Relief*, 125.

185. Ibid., 50.

186. Jean Wouters DiMotto, "Relaxation," *American Journal of Nursing* 84, No. 6 (June 1984), 757.

187. Robert Bolton, *People Skills, How To Assert Yourself, Listen To Others And Resolve Conflicts* (New York: Simon & Schuster, Inc., 1979), 211.

188. Ibid.

189. Jaffe and Scott, *From Burnout to Balance*, 35.

190. "Work-Related Stress Claims Are Expected To Skyrocket," *Labor Relations Week* 7 (October 20, 1993), 1013–1014.

191. Patricia S. Grant, "Manage Nurse Stress and Increase Potential at the Bedside," *Nursing Administration Quarterly* 18, No. 1 (Fall 1993), 16.

192. Dionne-Proulx and Pepin, "Stress Management," 79.

193. John Powell, *Why Am I Afraid To Tell You Who I Am?* (Niles, IL: Argus Communications, 1969), 43–44.

194. Ibid., 89.

195. Nathan et al., *Instant Stress Relief,* 152.

196. Ibid.

197. Sonya J. Herman, *Becoming Assertive: A Guide for Nurses* (New York: Van Nostrand Company, 1978), 17.

198. Melodie Chenevert, *STAT, Special Techniques in Assertiveness Training* (St. Louis: Mosby-Year Book, Inc., 1994), ix.

199. Gerry Angel and Diane Knox Petronko, *Developing the New Assertive Nurse: Essentials for Advancement* (New York: Springer Publishing Company, 1983), 8.

200. Ibid., 24.

201. Hamilton and Kiefer, *Survival Skills,* 227.

202. Angel and Petronko, *New Assertive Nurse,* 77–94.

203. Hamilton and Kiefer, *Survival Skills,* 14.

204. Mariann Johnson and Diana Gallagher, "Making Every Minute Count: Effective Time Management," *Imprint* 36, No. 3 (September/October 1989), 75.

205. Ibid.

206. Suzanne Carter, "Working Harder and Getting Nowhere—No Wonder You Are Stressed!" *Nursing Administration Quarterly* 18, No. 1 (Fall 1993), 51–52.

207. Hamilton and Kiefer, *Survival Skills,* 206.

208. Merrill E. Douglas and Phillip H. Goodwin, *Successful Time Management for Hospital Administrators* (New York: AMACOM, 1980), 56–57.

209. Elizabeth Arnold and Kathleen Boggs, *Interpersonal Relationships: Professional Communication Skills for Nurses* (Philadelphia: W. B. Saunders Co., 1989), 353.

210. Roe, "Conflict Management and Change," 89.

211. Shirley Steele, *Values Clarification in Nursing* (Norwalk, CT: Appleton-Century-Crofts, 1983), 3.

212. Suzanne Smith Coletta, "Values Clarification in Nursing: Why?" *American Journal of Nursing* 78, No. 12 (December 1978), 2057.

213. Karlene M. Kerfoot, "Managing by Values: The Nurse Manager's Challenge," *Nursing Economic$* 9, No. 3 (May-June 1991), 205.

214. Norton and Miller, *Skills for Professional Nursing Practice,* 31.

215. Sidney B. Simon, *Meeting Yourself Halfway—31 Values Clarification Strategies for Daily Living* (Niles, IL: Argus Communications, 1974), xv.

216. Hamilton and Kiefer, *Survival Skills,* 46.

217. Diane B. Uustal, "Values Clarification in Nursing: Application to Practice," *American Journal of Nursing* 78, No. 12 (December 1978), 2060.

218. Stephen R. Covey, *The Seven Habits of Highly Effective People, Personal Leadership Application Workbook* (New York: Simon & Schuster, 1989), 1.

219. Ibid.

220. Hamilton and Kiefer, *Survival Skills,* 52.

221. Ibid., 52–55.

222. Ibid., 51–52.

223. Ibid.

224. Uustal, "Values Certification in Nursing," 2059.

225. Ibid.

226. David B. Guralnik, ed., *Webster's New World Dictionary of the American Language* (New York: Simon & Schuster, 1982), 298.

227. Vicki D. Lachman, *Stress Management: A Manual for Nurses* (New York: Grune & Stratton, 1983), 119.

228. William Hendricks, *How To Manage Conflict, A Practical Guide to Effective Conflict Management* (Shawnee Mission, KS: National Press Publications, 1989), 6–12.

229. Ibid., 39–49.

230. Jaffe and Scott, *From Burnout to Balance,* 121.

231. Ibid.
232. Douglass, *The Effective Nurse*, 175–182.
233. Bolton, *People Skills*, 240.
234. Ibid.
235. Ibid., 239.
236. Douglass, *The Effective Nurse*, 175–176.
237. Ibid., 176.
238. Alan C. Filley, *Interpersonal Conflict Resolution* (Glenview, IL: Scott, Foresman, and Company, 1975), 25.
239. Douglass, *The Effective Nurse*, 176.
240. Bolton, *People Skills*, 218.
241. Ibid.
242. David W. Johnson, *Reaching Out—Interpersonal Effectiveness and Self-Actualization* (Englewood Cliffs, NJ: Prentice-Hall, 1981), 288–289.
243. Lachman, *Stress Management : A Manual for Nurses*, 130.
244. Arnold and Boggs, *Interpersonal Relationships: Professional Communication Skills for Nurses*, 60.
245. Hamilton and Kiefer, *Survival Skills*, 149.
246. William M. Warfel, "Communication in Complex Organizations," in *Management Concepts for the New Nurse*, ed. Katherine W. Vestal (Philadelphia: J. B. Lippincott, 1987), 38–39.
247. Angel and Petronko, *New Assertive Nurse*, 101.
248. Johnson, *Reaching Out—Interpersonal Effectiveness and Self-Actualization*, 80.
249. Angel and Petronko, *New Assertive Nurse*, 8.
250. Johnson, *Reaching Out—Interpersonal Effectiveness and Self-Actualization*, 79–80.
251. Bolton, *People Skills*, 118.
252. Ibid.
253. Stephen Cohen, "Assertiveness in Nursing: Part I," *American Journal of Nursing* 83, No. 3 (March 1983), 433.
254. Filley, *Interpersonal Conflict Resolution*, 41–42.
255. Robert L. Montgomery, *Listening Made Easy* (New York: American Management Association (AMACOM), 1981), 6.
256. Ibid., 8.
257. Margaret D. Sovie, "Redesigning Our Future: Whose Responsibility Is It?" *Nursing Economic$* 8, No. 1 (January/February 1990), 21.
258. "Chaos or Transformation? Managing Innovation," *Journal of Nursing Administration* 23, No. 5, 41.
259. Porter-O'Grady, "Transformational Leadership," 17.
260. Robert K. Merton, "Issues in the Growth of a Profession," *Summary of Proceedings of the 41st Convention of the American Nurses Association* (New York: American Nurses Association, 1958), 298.
261. JoEllen Goertz Koerner and Sandra Schmidt Bunkers, "Transformational Leadership: The Power of Symbol," *Nursing Administration Quarterly* 17, No. 1, 5.
262. Roe, "Conflict Management and Change," 103.
263. Lucie Young Kelly, *Dimensions of Professional Nursing* (New York: Macmillan Publishing Company, 1985), 361.
264. Irene Sabelburg Palmer, "Nightingale Revisited," *Nursing Outlook* 31, No. 4, 233.
265. George A. Flanagan, "Processing Grief," a presentation at the VA Medical Center, Kansas City, MO, April 1993.
266. Ronni Sandroff, "The Psychology of Change," *Working Woman*, July 1993, 54.
267. Ibid.
268. Angeline Bushy, "Managing Change: Strategies for Continuing Education," *Journal of Continuing Education in Nursing* 23, No. 5 (September/October 1992), 198.

269. Hershey and Blanchard, *Organizational Behavior,* 341.

270. Vogt and Murrell, *Empowerment in Organizations,* 139.

271. Roe, "Conflict Management and Change," 103.

272. Ibid.

273. Ibid.

274. Kelly, *Dimensions of Professional Nursing,* 360.

275. Roe, "Conflict Management and Change," 103.

276. Sandroff, "The Psychology of Change," 52.

277. Anita Gates, "A Guide to Changing Careers in the 90s," *Working Woman,* April 1992, 58.

278. Wendy Leebov, *Job Satisfaction Strategies for Health Care Professionals* (Chicago: American Hospital Publishing, 1991), 20.

279. "Strategic Directions to Maintain Registered Nurses as the Key Component in Quality Patient Care Today and into the Future," *Summary of Proceedings, 1994 ANA House of Delegates,* 64.

280. Ibid.

281. Ibid.

282. Sandroff, "The Psychology of Change," 56.

283. Barry B. Grossman and Ray J. Blitzer, "Choreographing Careers," *Training & Development,* January 1992, 68.

284. Lyndia Flanagan, *Entering and Moving in the Professional Job Market: A Nurse's Resource Kit* (Kansas City, MO: American Nurses Association, 1988), 13.

285. Jill L. Sherer, "How Safe Is Your Job?" *Hospitals & Health Networks* 68, No. 7 (April 5, 1994), 49.

286. Ibid.

287. Lyndia Flanagan, *Entering and Moving in the Professional Job Market,* 13.

288. Bolton, *People Skills,* 7.

289. David B. Guralnik, *Webster's New World Dictionary* (New York: Simon & Schuster, 1982), 952.

290. Jo Manion, *Change from Within, Nurse Intrapreneurs as Health Care Innovators* (Kansas City, MO: American Nurses Association, 1990), 39.

291. American Nurses Association, *Local Unit Handbook,* 64.

292. M. Susan Grossa Law, Marion Oare Smith, Sharon Norman Igoe, and Marcy S. Caplin, "Nurses Helping Nurses," *Imprint,* April/May 1989, 67.

293. Anne Baber and Lynne Waymon, *Great Connections, Small Talk and Networking for Businesspeople* (Manassas Park, VA: Impact Publications, 1992), 134.

294. Ibid.

295. Ibid., 136.

296. Ibid., 2.

297. Ibid., 4.

298. Suzanne D. Holloran, "Mentoring, The Experience of Nursing Service Executives," *Journal of Nursing Administration* 23, No. 2 (February 1993), 49.

299. Connie N. Vance, "The Mentor Connection," *Journal of Nursing Administration* 12, No. 4 (April 1982), 8.

300. Hamilton and Kiefer, *Survival Skills,* 165.

301. Judith K. Leavitt and Camille Barry, "Learning The Ropes," *Imprint,* September/October 1993, 59.

302. Ibid.

303. Law et al., "Nurses Helping Nurses," 71.

304. Holloran, "Mentoring," 51.

BIBLIOGRAPHY

Ackoff, Russell L. 1989. The Circular Organization: An Update. *Academy of Management Executive*, February, 7–16.

A Decade of Change: AHA's Annual Survey Traces National Trends, 1980–1990. 1991. *Hospitals* 65, No. 24, 32–36.

Albrecht, Terrance L. 1982. What Job Stress Means for the Staff Nurse. *Nursing Administration Quarterly* 7, No. 1, 3–5.

Alexander Hamilton Institute. 1991. *What Every Manager Must Know to Prevent Sexual Harassment*. Maywood, NJ: the Institute.

Alward, Ruth R. and Timothy H. Monk. 1993. *The Nurse's Shift Work Handbook*. Washington, DC: American Nurses Publishing.

American Nurses Association. 1994. ADVISORY: Total Quality Management (TQM), Continuous Quality Improvement (CQI), Joint Governance.

_____. 1994. *Every Patient Deserves a Nurse*. Washington, DC: the Association.

_____. 1993. Fact Sheet on the Family and Medical Leave Act (FMLA) of 1993.

_____. 1994. *Guidelines on Reporting Incompetent, Unethical or Illegal Practices*. Washington, DC: the Association.

_____. 1994. Health Care Layoffs: Developing a Strategic Plan from the State Nurses Association Perspective. ANA, Washington, DC.

_____. 1992. *HIV, Hepatitis-B, Hepatitis-C Bloodborne Diseases—Nurses' Risks, Rights, and Responsibilities*. Washington, DC: the Association.

_____. 1994. How Do You Know . . . If Your Paycheck Is Correct? Washington, DC: the Association.

_____. 1989. *How to Organize a Collective Bargaining Unit*. Kansas City, MO: the Association.

_____. 1992. *Liability Prevention & You, What Nurses & Employers Need to Know*. Washington, DC: the Association.

_____. 1993. *Local Unit Handbook, a Basic Resource for SNA Bargaining Units*. Washington, DC: the Association.

_____. 1994. *Nursing and HIV/AIDS*. Washington, DC: American Nurses Publishing.

_____. 1992. *Nursing's Agenda for Health Care Reform*. Kansas City, MO: American Nurses Publishing.

_____. 1993. Peer Support for the HIV-Positive Nurse, a Guide for the Development of Programs and Materials.

_____. 1993. Position Statement on Sexual Harassment.

_____. 1993. Registered Nurses: A Distinctive Health Care Profession, Nursing Facts. Washington, DC: American Nurses Publishing.

_____. 1994. *Registered Professional Nurses and Unlicensed Assistive Personnel*. Washington, DC: American Nurses Publishing.

_____. 1993. *Sexual Harassment, It's against the Law*. Washington, DC: the Association.

_____. 1993. *Tuberculosis, a Deadly Disease Makes a Comeback*. Washington, DC: the Association.

American Nurses Foundation. 1993. *America's Nurses: An Untapped Natural Resource, Business Solutions for Health Care Delivery*. Washington, DC: the Foundation.

Anderson, Howard J. 1992. Hospitals Seek New Ways to Integrate Health Care. *Hospitals* 66, No. 7, 26–36.

Anderson, Howard J. 1993. New Planning Models, Reasons for Transforming Hospitals Go Beyond Financials. *Hospitals* 67, No. 3, 20–22.

Angel, Gerry and Diane Knox Petronko. 1983. *Developing the New Assertive Nurse: Essentials for Advancement.* New York: Springer Publishing Company.

Arnold, Elizabeth and Kathleen Boggs. 1989. *Interpersonal Relationships: Professional Communication Skills for Nurses.* Philadelphia: W. B. Saunders Company.

Aurelio, Jeanne M. 1993. An Organizational Culture That Optimizes Stress: Acceptable Stress in Nursing. *Nursing Administration Quarterly* 18, No. 1, 1–10.

Austin-Lett, Genelle and Jan Sprague. 1976. *Talk to Yourself, Experiencing Intrapersonal Communication.* Boston: Houghton Mifflin Company.

Baber, Anne and Lynne Waymon. 1992. *Great Connections, Small Talk and Networking for Businesspeople.* Manassas Park, VA: Impact Publications.

Batten, Joe. 1992. *Building a Total Quality Culture.* Menlo Park, CA: Crisp Publications, Inc.

Bennis, Warren and Burt Nanus. 1985. *Leaders—The Strategies for Taking Charge.* New York: Harper & Row.

Bergman, Rhonda. 1994. Reengineering Health Care. *Hospitals & Health Networks* 68, No. 3, 28–32.

Berne, Eric. 1964. *Games People Play.* New York: Ballantine Books.

Blanchard, Kenneth, Donald Carew, and Eunice Parisi-Carew. 1990. *The One-Minute Manager Builds High Performing Teams.* New York: William Morrow & Company, Inc.

Bloch, Gordon Bakoulis. 1992. Stress Signals. *Working Woman,* February, 80–81.

BNA Plus Research. 1990. *The Future of Work & Family: Shaping Programs for the 21st Century.* Washington, DC: The Bureau of National Affairs.

Bolton, Robert. 1979. People Skills, *How to Assert Yourself, Listen to Others, and Resolve Conflicts.* New York: Simon & Schuster, Inc.

Bostrom, Janet and Joann Zimmerman. 1993. Restructuring Nursing for a Competitive Health Care Environment. *Nursing Economic$* 11, No. 1, 35–41.

Boyett, Joseph H. and Henry P. Conn. 1991. *Workplace 2000, the Revolution Reshaping American Business.* New York: Penguin Books.

Breakwell, Glynis M. 1990. Are You Stressed Out? *American Journal of Nursing* 90, No. 8, 31–33.

Brewer, Kristine C. 1991. *The Stress Management Handbook.* Shawnee Mission, KS: National Press Publications.

Buckley, Catherine D. and Diane Walker. 1989. *Harmony: Professional Renewal for Nurses.* Chicago, IL: American Hospital Publishing.

Buerhaus, Peter I. 1992. Nursing, Competition, and Quality. *Nursing Economic$* 10, No. 1, 21–29.

Bushy, Angeline. 1992. Managing Change: Strategies for Continuing Education. *Journal of Continuing Education in Nursing* 23, No. 5, 197–208.

Cairo, Jim. 1990. *Motivation & Goal-Setting: The Keys to Achieving Success.* Shawnee Mission, KS: National Press Publications.

Carey, Raymond G. and Jerry H. Seibert. 1993. A Patient Survey System to Measure Quality Improvement: Questionnaire Reliability and Validity. *Medical Care* 31, No. 9, 834–845.

Carter, Suzanne. 1993. Working Harder and Getting Nowhere—No Wonder You Are Stressed! *Nursing Administration Quarterly* 18, No. 1, 51–55.

Chapman, JoAnn. 1993. Collegial Support Linked to Reduction of Job Stress. *Nursing Management* 24, No. 5, 52–56.

Chenevert, Melodie. 1994. *STAT, Special Techniques in Assertiveness Training.* St. Louis: Mosby-Year Book, Inc.

_____. 1993. *The Pro-Nurse Handbook, Designed for the Nurse Who Wants to Thrive Professionally.* St. Louis: Mosby-Year Book, Inc.

Coletta, Suzanne Smith. 1978. Values Clarification in Nursing: Why? *American Journal of Nursing* 78, No. 12, 2057.

Cornell, Dixie. 1993. Say the Words: Communication Techniques. *Nursing Management* 24, No. 3, 42–44.

Covey, Stephen R. 1989. *The Seven Habits of Highly Effective People, Personal Leadership Application Workbook*. New York: Simon & Schuster.

Davidson, Dick. 1992. A Decade of Competition Ends—A New Era of Cooperation Begins. *Hospitals* 66, No. 2, 44–46, 48.

Davidson, Eleanor. 1991. Communicating with a Diverse Workforce. *Supervisory Management* 36, No. 12, 1–2.

DeVries, Christine M. and Marjorie W. Vanderbilt. 1992. *The Grassroots Lobbying Handbook*. Washington, DC: American Nurses Publishing.

Dewey, John. 1963. *How We Think*. Boston: D. C. Heath & Company.

Dienemann, Jacqueline, ed. 1992. *C.Q.I.—Continuous Quality Improvement in Nursing*. Washington, DC: American Nurses Publishing.

_____. 1993. Share Ideas to Speed CQI Success. *The American Nurse* 25, No. 1, 4, 17.

Dienemann, Jacqueline and Theodore Gessner. 1992. Restructuring Nursing Care Delivery Systems. *Nursing Economic$* 10, No. 4, 253–258.

DiMotto, Jean Wouters. 1984. Relaxation. *American Journal of Nursing* 84, No. 6, 754–758.

Dionne-Proulx, J. and R. Pepin. 1993. Stress Management in the Nursing Profession. *Journal of Nursing Management* 1, 75–81.

Douglass, Laura Mae. 1984. *The Effective Nurse—Leader and Manager*. St. Louis: C. V. Mosby.

Douglas, Merrill E. and Phillip H. Goodwin. 1980. *Successful Time Management for Hospital Administrators*. New York: AMACOM.

Eubanks, Paula. 1992. The New Nurse Manager: A Linchpin in Quality Care and Cost Control. *Hospitals* 66, No. 8, 22–29.

_____. 1992. Work Redesign Calls for New Pay and Performance Plans. *Hospitals* 66, No. 19, 56, 58, 60.

Family and Medical Leave Act Regulations. 1993. *Union Labor Report* 47, No. 23, 5.

Farley, Mary J. 1992. Thought and Talk, The Intrapersonal Component of Human Communication. *AORN Journal* 56, No. 3, 481–484.

Filley, Alan C. 1975. *Interpersonal Conflict Resolution*. Glenview, IL: Scott, Foresman, and Company.

Flanagan, Lyndia. 1988. *Entering and Moving in the Professional Job Market: A Nurse's Resource Kit*. Kansas City, MO: American Nurses Association.

_____. 1993. The Hospital Industry: A Decade of Change. *E&GW Update* 11, No. 1, 1–39.

Flarey, Dominick L. 1991. The Social Climate Scale, A Tool for Organizational Change and Development. *Journal of Nursing Administration* 21, No. 4, 37–44.

French, Ellen and Ramon Lavandero, eds. 1990. *Nursing Recruitment & Retention, Strategies That Work*. Laguna Niguel, CA: American Association of Critical-Care Nurses.

Friedman, Emily. 1991. Health Care's Changing Face: The Demographics of the 21st Century. *Hospitals* 65, No. 7, 36–40.

Gardner, Elizabeth. 1992. R.N. Meets T.Q.M. *Modern Healthcare*, October 5, 35.

Gastel, Barbara. 1993. Hospitals and Hospitals: Evolving Together. *Hospitals* 67, No. 10, 64.

Gates, Anita. 1992. A Guide to Changing Careers in the 90s. *Working Woman*, April, 57–60.

Grainger, Ruth Dailey. 1990. Anger within Ourselves. *American Journal of Nursing* 90, No. 7, 12.

_____. 1990. Anxiety Interrupters. *American Journal of Nursing* 90, No. 2, 14–15.

_____. 1992. Are You Overreacting? *American Journal of Nursing* 92, No. 3, 11–12.

_____. 1992. Beating Burnout. *American Journal of Nursing* 92, No. 1, 15, 17.

_____. 1991. Managing Stress. *American Journal of Nursing* 91, No. 9, 15–16.

_____. 1990. Successful Grieving. *American Journal of Nursing* 90, No. 9, 12–13.

Greene, Jay. 1992. Hospitals Now Merge Rather Than Close. *Modern Healthcare*, July 6, 20, 22.

Grossman, Divina. 1994. Enhancing Your Cultural Competence. *American Journal of Nursing* 94, No. 7, 61–62.

Hamilton, Jane Meier and Marcy E. Kiefer. 1986. *Survival Skills for the New Nurse.* Philadelphia: J. B. Lippincott.

Hamilton, Jim. 1993. Toppling the Power of the Pyramid. *Hospitals* 67, No. 1, 38–41.

Hastings, Clare, Sharon O'Keefe, and Janet Buckley. 1992. Professional Practice Partnerships: A New Approach to Creating High Performance Nursing Organizations. *Nursing Administration Quarterly* 17, No. 1, 45–54.

Havens, Donna Sullivan. 1992. Nursing Involvement in Hospital Governance: 1990 and 1995. *Nursing Economic$* 10, No.5, 331–335.

Hendricks, William. 1989. *How to Manage Conflict, a Practical Guide to Effective Conflict Management.* Shawnee Mission, KS: National Press Publications.

Herman, Sonya J. 1978. *Becoming Assertive: A Guide for Nurses.* New York: Van Nostrand Company.

Herrmann, John. 1990. New Strategies—Managing Hospitals in the 90s. *Federation of American Health Systems Review*, July/August, 14–23.

Herron, Dorothy G. and Lanny Herron. 1991. Entrepreneurial Nursing as a Conceptual Basis for In-Hospital Nursing Practice Models. *Nursing Economic$* 9, No. 5, 310–316.

Hershey, Paul and Kenneth H. Blanchard 1988. *Management of Organizational Behavior, Utilizing Human Resources.* Englewood Cliffs, NJ: Prentice-Hall.

Hicks, Lanis L., Janet M. Stallmeyer, and John R. Coleman. 1993. *Role of the Nurse in Managed Care.* Washington, DC: American Nurses Publishing.

Holloran, Suzanne D. 1993. Mentoring, The Experience of Nursing Service Executives. *Journal of Nursing Administration* 23, No. 2, 49–54.

Hunt, James W. 1988. *The Law of the Workplace: Rights of Employers and Employees.* Washington, DC: The Bureau of National Affairs.

Gallagher, Diana Lynn. 1989. Is Stress Ripping Nurses Apart? *Imprint* 36, No. 2, 59–63.

Grant, Patricia S. 1993. Manage Nurse Stress and Increase Potential at the Bedside. *Nursing Administration Quarterly* 18, No. 1, 16–22.

Imundo, Louis V. 1992. Blueprint for a Successful Team. *Supervisory Management*, May, 2–3.

Integrated Care: A Look Inside Tomorrow's Hospital. 1992. *Hospitals* 66, No. 4, 47–50.

Jablonski, Joseph R. 1992. *Implementing TQM—Competing in the Nineties through Total Quality Management.* Albuquerque, NM: Technical Management Consortium.

Jaffe, Dennis T. and Cynthia D. Scott. 1984. *From Burnout to Balance, a Workbook for Peak Performance and Self Renewal.* New York: McGraw-Hill Book Company.

Jensen, Donna Buchanan. 1993. Interpretation of Group Behavior. *Nursing Management* 24, No. 3, 49–54.

Johnson, David W. 1981. *Interpersonal Effectiveness and Self-Actualization.* Englewood Cliffs, NJ: Prentice-Hall.

Johnson, Julie. 1992. Managed Care in the 1990s: Providers' New Role for Innovative Health Delivery. *Hospitals* 66, No. 6, 26–30.

Johnson, Mariann and Diana Gallagher. 1989. Making Every Minute Count: Effective Time Management. *Imprint* 36, No. 3, 75.

Kanter, Rosabeth Moss. 1989. *When Giants Learn to Dance—Mastering the Challenges of Strategy, Management, and Careers in the 1990s.* New York: Simon and Schuster.

Kaufman, Nathan. 1994. Eight Guidelines for Developing a Strategy for the 90s. *Hospitals & Health Networks* 68, No. 6, 78.

Kelly, Lucie Young. 1985. *Dimensions of Professional Nursing.* New York: Macmillan Publishing Company.

_____. 1987. *The Nursing Experience—Trends, Challenges, and Transitions.* New York: Macmillan Publishing Company.

Kerfoot, Karlene M. 1991. Managing by Values: The Nurse Manager's Challenge. *Nursing Economic$* 9, No. 3, 205–206, 214.

Ketter, Joni. 1994. ANA: Protecting Nurses and Patient Care in the Face of Restructuring. *The American Nurse* 26, No. 5, 1.

_____. 1994. Surviving Layoffs. *The American Nurse* 26, No. 7, 25.

_____. 1994. When 1+1=1, How 'Merger Mania' Is Impacting Nurses Across America. *The American Nurse* 26, No. 7, 22, 24.

Koerner, JoEllen Goertz and Sandra Schmidt Bunkers. 1992. Transformational Leadership: The Power of Symbol. *Nursing Administration Quarterly* 17, No. 1, 1–9.

Kouzes, James M. and Barry Z. Posner. 1987. *The Leadership Challenges, How to Get Extraordinary Things Done in Organizations.* San Francisco: Jossey-Bass Publishers.

Kramer, Marlene. 1974. *Reality Shock: Why Nurses Leave Nursing.* St. Louis: C. V. Mosby.

Kramer, Marlene and Laurin P. Hafner. 1989. Shared Values: Impact on Staff Nurse Job Satisfaction and Perceived Productivity. *Nursing Research* 38, No. 3, 172–177.

Lachman, Vicki D. 1983. *Stress Management: A Manual for Nurses.* New York: Grune & Stratton.

Lajkowicz, Christine. 1993. Teaching Cultural Diversity for the Workplace. *Journal of Nursing Education* 32, No. 5, 235–236.

Larson, Carl E. and Frank M. J. LaFasto. 1989. *TeamWork—What Must Go Right/What Can Go Wrong.* New York: Sage Publications.

Law, M. Susan Grossa, Marion Oare Smith, Sharon Norman Igoe, and Marcy S. Caplin. 1989. Nurses Helping Nurses. *Imprint* 36, No. 3, 65–72.

Lawler, Edward E. 1988. *High Involvement Management.* San Francisco: Jossey-Bass Publishers.

Leebov, Wendy. 1991. *Job Satisfaction Strategies for Health Care Professionals.* Chicago: American Hospital Publishing, Inc.

Luft, Joseph. 1984. *Group Process, an Introduction to Group Dynamics.* Palo Alto, CA: Mayfield Publishing Company.

Lumsdon, Kevin. 1993. Form Follows Function, Patient-Centered Care Needs Strong Facilities Planning. *Hospitals* 67, No. 3, 22–26.

_____. 1992. HIV-Positive Health Care Workers Pose Legal, Safety Challenges for Hospitals. *Hospitals* 66, No. 18, 24–32.

Lutz, Sandy. 1993. Hospitals Continue Move into Home Care. *Modern Healthcare*, January 25, 28–32.

_____. 1992. Hospitals Gird to Fight 'Disease of the Future.' *Modern Healthcare*, December 7, 22–24, 26, 28.

McCloskey, Joanne and Helen K. Grace. 1994. *Current Issues in Nursing.* St. Louis: Mosby-Year Book, Inc.

McKibbin, Richard C. 1990. *The Nursing Shortage and the 1990s: Realities and Remedies.* Kansas City, MO: American Nurses Association.

McNamara, Rosalee M. 1994. Court Decision Narrowed Outline of Harassment. *The Kansas City Star*, March 22, D-18.

Mallison, Mary B. 1992. How Nurses Redefine Reality. *American Journal of Nursing* 92, No. 5, 7.

Mallory, Charles. 1991. *Team-Building, How to Build a "Winning" Team.* Shawnee Mission, KS: National Press Publications.

Manganelli, Raymond and Mark M. Klein. 1994. A Framework for Reengineering. *Management Review*, June, 10–16.

Manion, Jo. 1990. *Change from Within, Nurse Intrapreneurs as Health Care Innovators.* Kansas City, MO: American Nurses Association.

_____. 1993. Chaos or Transformation? Managing Innovation. *Journal of Nursing Administration* 23, No. 5, 41–48.

Maslow, Abraham H. 1987. *Motivation and Personality.* New York: Harper & Row Publishers, Inc.

Minnen, Terry G., Elizabeth Burger, Adrienne Ames, Marilyn Dubree, Wendy L. Baker, and Judy Spinella. 1993. Sustaining Work Redesign Innovations through Shared Governance. *Journal of Nursing Administration* 23, No. 7/8, 35–40.

Montgomery, Robert L. 1981. *Listening Made Easy.* New York: American Management Association.

Murphy, Catherine P. and Howard Hunter. 1983. *Ethical Problems in the Nurse-Patient Relationship.* Newton, MA: Allyn & Bacon.

Nathan, Ronald G., Thomas E. Staats, and Paul J. Rosch. 1987. *The Doctor's Guide to Instant Stress Relief.* New York: Ballantine Books.

Norton, Barbara A. and Anna M. Miller. 1986. *Skills for Professional Nursing Practice.* Norwalk, CT: Appleton-Century-Crofts.

Nyberg, Jan. 1991. The Nurse as Professsnocrat. *Nursing Economic$* 9, No. 4, 244–247.

O'Connor, Andrea B. 1982. Ingredients for Successful Networking. *Journal of Nursing Administration* 12, No. 11, 36–40.

OSHA Chief: A New Voice on Safety—Joseph A. Dear. 1994. *Hospitals & Health Networks* 68, No. 13, 55.

OSHA Reform Legislation. 1994. *Capital Update* 12, No. 6, 2.

Palmer, Irene Sabelberg. 1983. Nightingale Revisited. *Nursing Outlook* 31, No. 4, 229–233.

Peregrine, Michael W. and James W. Teevans. 1992. New Focus on Efficiencies Emerges in Merger Review. *Health Law Reporter*, October 15, 139–142.

Peters, Tom. 1987. *Thriving on Chaos, Handbook for a Management Revolution.* New York: Alfred A. Knopf, Inc.

Peters, Tom and Nancy Austin. 1985. *A Passion for Excellence, the Leadership Difference.* New York: Random House.

Pines, Ayala and Elliot Aronson. 1988. *Career Burnout Causes and Cures.* New York: The Free Press.

Policies and Benefits Supportive of Working Parents. 1986. *E&GW Update* 4, No. 10, 4–6.

Popcorn, Faith. 1992. *The Popcorn Report.* New York: Harper Business.

Porter-O'Grady, Tim. 1986. *Creative Nursing Administration: Participative Management into the 21st Century.* Rockville, MD: Aspen Systems Corporation.

_____. 1992. Transformational Leadership in an Age of Chaos. *Nursing Administration Quarterly* 17, No. 1, 17–24.

Powell, John. 1969. *Why Am I Afraid to Tell You Who I Am?* Niles, IL: Argus Communications.

Prescott, Patricia A. 1993. Nursing: An Important Component of Hospital Survival under a Reformed Health Care System. *Nursing Economic$* 11, No. 4, 192–199.

Prim, Roberta G. 1991. Communication: Coping with the Unspoken Dance. *Nursing Management* 24, No. 3, 33–35.

Rabinowitz, Randy. 1992. *Is Your Job Making You Sick? A CLUW Handbook on Workplace Hazards.* New York: Coalition of Labor Union Women.

Roberson, Mildred. 1993. Defining Cultural and Ethnic Differences to Adapt to a Changing Patient Population. *The American Nurse* 25, No. 8. 6.

Rogers, Carl R. 1961. *On Becoming a Person.* Boston: Houghton Mifflin Company.

Rowland, Howard S. and Beatrice L. Rowland. 1984. *Hospital Administration Handbook.* Rockville, MD: Aspen Systems Corporation.

Russo, J. Edward and Paul J. H. Schoemaker. 1989. *Decision Traps, the Ten Barriers to Brilliant Decision-Making and How to Overcome Them.* New York: Bantam Doubleday Dell Publishing Group, Inc.

Sandroff, Ronni. 1993. The Psychology of Change. *Working Woman*, July, 52–56.

Sashkin, Marshall and Kenneth J. Kiser. 1993. *Putting Total Quality Management to Work.* San Francisco: Berrett-Koehler Publishers.

Schul, Bill D. 1975. *How to Be an Effective Group Leader.* Chicago: Nelson-Hall.

Selby, Terry. 1992. Nurses Face Growing Risk of Violence and Abuse. *The American Nurse* 24, No. 4, 3.

Selye, Hans. 1974. *Stress without Distress.* New York: Signet.

_____. 1976. *The Stress of Life.* New York: McGraw.

Senge, Peter M. 1990. *The Fifth Discipline, The Art and Practice of the Learning Organization.* New York: Doubleday/Currency.

Sessa, Valerie I., Jo Anne Bennett, and Carole Birdsall. 1993. Conflict with Less Distress: Promoting Team Effectiveness. *Nursing Administration Quarterly* 18, No. 1, 57–65.

Sherer, Jill L. 1993. Changing Cultures, Hospital Staffs Get Used to Patient-Centered Care Plans. *Hospitals* 67, No. 3, 18–19.

_____. 1993. Putting Patients First, Hospitals Work to Define Patient-Centered Care. *Hospitals* 67, No. 3, 14–18.

_____. 1993. Will Health Care Reform Rewrite Nursing's Role? *Hospitals* 67, No. 8, reprint.

Simon, Sidney B. 1974. *Meeting Yourself Halfway—31 Values Clarification Strategies for Daily Living.* Niles, IL: Argus Communications.

Skinner, Kathryn and R. Dianne Scott. 1993. Depression among Female Registered Nurses. *Nursing Management* 24, No. 8, 42–45.

Smythe, Emily E. M. 1984. *Surviving Nursing.* Menlo Park, CA: Addision-Wesley.

Solomon, Muriel. 1990. *Working with Difficult People.* Englewood Cliffs, NJ: Prentice-Hall.

Solovy, Alden T. 1993. Retooling the Hospital: Moving into the Second Phase. *Hospitals* 67, No. 5, 18–19.

Souhrada, Laura. 1991. Hospitals' Use of Contract Management Approaches 50%. *Hospitals* 65, No. 3, 18–20, 22, 24.

Sovie, Margaret D. 1993. Hospital Culture—Why Create One? *Nursing Economic$* 11, No. 2, 69–75, 90.

_____. 1990. Redesigning Our Future: Whose Responsibility Is It? *Nursing Economic$* 8, No. 1, 21–26.

Steele, Shirley. 1983. *Values Clarification in Nursing.* Norwalk, CT: Appleton-Century-Crofts.

Stevens, Barbara J. 1985. *The Nurse as Executive.* Rockville, MD: Aspen Publishers.

Styles, Margretta M. 1982. *On Nursing—Toward a New Endowment.* St. Louis, MO: C. V. Mosby Company.

Supreme Court Issues Fragmented Ruling on Free Speech Rights of Public Employees. 1994. *Government Employee Relations Report* 32, No. 1568, 20.

The Bureau of National Affairs, Inc. 1987. *Stress in the Workplace: Costs, Liability, and Prevention.* Rockville, MD: the Bureau.

_____. 1989. *Occupational Safety and Health: Seven Critical Issues for the 1990s.* Rockville, MD: the Bureau.

_____. 1992. *Preventing Sexual Harassment, a Fact Sheet for Employees.* Rockville, MD: BNA Books.

The 3M Meeting Management Team. 1979. *How to Run Better Business Meetings: A Reference Guide for Managers.* New York: McGraw-Hill.

Tompkins, Emily S. 1992. Nurse/Client Values Congruence. *Western Journal of Nursing Research* 14, No. 2, 225–236.

Understanding the Americans with Disabilities Act, a Fact Sheet for Employees. 1993. *Union Labor Report,* 47, No. 14, 1–8.

U.S. Department of Labor, Occupational Safety and Health Administration. 1991. *Ergonomics: The Study of Work.* Washington, DC: U.S. Government Printing Office.

U.S. Department of Labor, Office of the Secretary, Women's Bureau. 1989. *Work and Family Resource Kit.* Washington, DC: U.S. Government Printing Office.

Uustal, Diane B. 1978. Values Clarification in Nursing: Application to Practice. *American Journal of Nursing* 78, No. 12, 2058–2063.

Vance, Connie N. 1982. The Mentor Connection. *Journal of Nursing Administration* 12, No. 4, 8.

Vestal, Katherine W., ed. 1987. *Management Concepts for the New Nurse*. Philadelphia: J. B. Lippincott.

Vogt, Judith F. and Kenneth L. Murrell. 1990. *Empowerment in Organizations, How to Spark Exceptional Performance*. San Diego, CA: University Associates, Inc.

Wagner, Ellen J. 1992. *Sexual Harassment in the Workplace, How to Prevent, Investigate, and Resolve Problems in Your Organization*. New York: Creative Solutions, Inc.

WARN Amendments Give Added Protection to Nurses. 1994. *The American Nurse* 26, No. 7, 25.

Ways to Develop Your Cultural Sensitivity. 1993. *The American Nurse* 25, No. 8, 16.

What Restructuring May Mean to Nurses. 1994. *The American Nurse* 26, No. 5, 1, 14.

Wieseke, Ann and Diana Bantz. 1992. Economic Awareness of Registered Nurses. *Nursing Economic$* 10, No. 6, 406–412.

Williams, Peggy S. 1989. Physical Fitness for Committees: Getting on Track. *Association Management* 41, No. 6, 105–111.

Woodhouse, Diana Kenney. 1993. The Aspects of Humor in Dealing with Stress. *Nursing Administration Quarterly* 18, No. 1, 80–89.

Worthington, Karen. 1993. Taking Action against Violence in the Workplace. *The American Nurse* 25, No. 6, 12.

_____. 1994. Workplace Hazards: The Effect on Nurses as Women. *The American Nurse* 26, No. 2, 15.

Yalom, Irwin D. 1985. *The Theory and Practice of Group Psychotherapy*. New York: Basic Books.